Hands-On Financial Modeling with Microsoft Excel 2019

Build practical models for forecasting, valuation, trading, and growth analysis using Excel 2019

Shmuel Oluwa

BIRMINGHAM - MUMBAI

Hands-On Financial Modeling with Microsoft Excel 2019

Commissioning Editor: Pavan Ramchandani
Acquisition Editor: Yogesh Deokar
Content Development Editor: Nathanya Dias
Senior Editor: Martin Whittemore
Technical Editor: Joseph Sunil
Copy Editor: Safis Editing
Project Coordinator: Kirti Pisat
Proofreader: Safis Editing
Indexer: Priyanka Dhadke
Production Designer: Jyoti Chauhan

First published: July 2019

Production reference: 1080719

Published by Packt Publishing Ltd.
Livery Place
35 Livery Street
Birmingham
B3 2PB, UK.

ISBN 978-1-78953-462-7

www.packtpub.com

I would like to thank the Almighty God for this opportunity to express myself beyond the lecture room and for guiding me through this, my first book.

My gratitude goes to Paramdeep Singh, whose effortless genius in all its MP4 glory first introduced me to a topic that has become a passion; Pawan Prabhat for his faith in me on very little evidence; and Rupinder Monga for his guidance and encouragement in the early years.

I am grateful to the numerous students who have insisted on rating me highly when I know I deserved less. I cannot express how much your words of approval have meant to me.

To Reshma, who first reached out to me about writing this book; Nathanya, for your endless patience and words of encouragement; Gebin, for the wake-up call; and everyone at Packt for this priceless opportunity. I cannot thank you enough.

Finally, my immense gratitude goes to my family and friends, without whose support this would not have been possible. My dear wife, Imiel, for her patience and tolerance; my wonderful daughter, Eligadel; and my grandson, Hoshiyahu; I am truly blessed to have you; my siblings, Tunde and Sassonel, the bond between us is as reassuring as it is rewarding. I can do no wrong in your eyes.

Last but not least, my good friend, Eliyatser, and my tolerant assistant, Bosede; your words of encouragement have gone much further than you could have imagined.

Contributors

About the author

Shmuel Oluwa is a financial executive and seasoned instructor with over 25 years' experience in a number of finance-related fields, with a passion for imparting knowledge. He has developed considerable skills in the use of Microsoft Excel and has organized training courses in Business Excel, Financial Modeling with Excel, Forensics and Fraud Detection with Excel, Excel as an Investigative Tool, and Accounting for Non-Accountants, among others. He has given classes in Nigeria, Angola, Kenya, and Tanzania, but his online community of students covers several continents.

Shmuel divides his time between London and Lagos with his pharmacist wife. He is fluent in three languages: English, Yoruba, and Hebrew.

I would like to dedicate this book to my late parents, Yirael and Levi Oluwa, and to my beloved late sister, Hodel Oluwa. Only the memories can soften the loss.

About the reviewers

Bernard Obeng Boateng is a data analyst and a financial modeler with over 10 years' working experience in banking, insurance, and business development. He has a BSc degree in administration from the University of Ghana Business School, and is certified in business analytics from the world's leading business school, Wharton. Bernard is the principal consultant of BEST LTD, a firm that provides training and financial solutions to individuals and corporate institutions in Ghana.

As a financial modeler, he was part of a team that created an agriculture insurance risk model for the governments of Ghana and Rwanda. He has trained over 500 hundred corporate workers in Ghana and has an online training video series called *Excel Hacks for Productivity*.

Tony De Jonker, Excel Microsoft MVP is the principal of De Jonker Consultancy and AlwaysExcel, The Netherlands and specializes in Financial Modeling, Analysis, Reporting and Training for clients worldwide. He is the founder and presenter of the annual Excel events, such as Excel Experience Day, Excel Expert Class and Amsterdam Excel BI Summit. Tony offers a range of Excel Business related training courses in Dutch, English or German based on more than 34 years of spreadsheet modeling and more than 41 years of Finance and Accounting experience. and has written more than 150 articles on using Excel in Business for the Dutch Controller's Magazine.

Packt is searching for authors like you

If you're interested in becoming an author for Packt, please visit `authors.packtpub.com` and apply today. We have worked with thousands of developers and tech professionals, just like you, to help them share their insight with the global tech community. You can make a general application, apply for a specific hot topic that we are recruiting an author for, or submit your own idea.

Table of Contents

Section 2: The Use of Excel - Features and Functions for Financial Modeling

Section 3: Building an Integrated Financial Model

Preface

Financial modeling is a core skill required by anyone who wants to build a career in finance. *Hands-On Financial Modeling with Microsoft Excel 2019* examines various definitions and relates them to the key features of financial modeling with the help of Excel.

This book will help you understand financial modeling concepts using Excel, and provides you with an overview of the steps you should follow to build an integrated financial model. You will explore the design principles, functions, and techniques of building models in a practical manner. Starting with the key concepts of Excel, such as formulas and functions, you will learn about referencing frameworks and other advanced components of Excel for building financial models. Later chapters will help you understand your financial projects, build assumptions, and analyze historical data to develop data-driven models and functional growth drivers. The book takes an intuitive approach to model testing, along with best practices and practical use cases.

By the end of this book, you will have examined the data from various use cases, and you will have the skills you need to build financial models to extract the information required to make informed business decisions.

Who this book is for

This book is for data professionals, analysts, and traders, as well as business owners and students, who want to implement the skill of financial modeling in their analysis, trading, and valuation work and develop a highly in-demand skill in finance. The book assumes a working knowledge of Excel.

What this book covers

Chapter 1, *Introduction to Financial Modeling and Excel*, shows you the basic ingredients of a financial model and what are my favorite definitions of a financial model. You will also learn about the different tools for financial modeling that currently exist in the industry, as well as those features of Excel that make it the ideal tool to use in order to handle the various needs of a financial model.

Chapter 2, *Steps for Building a Financial Model*, helps you to devise a systematic plan to observe that will allow you or any other user to follow the flow from the beginning to the end of your model. It will also facilitate the building of your model and provide a useful roadmap for troubleshooting any errors or discrepancies that may arise.

Chapter 3, *Formulas and Functions – Completing Modeling Tasks with a Single Formula*, teaches you the difference between formulas and functions. You will learn the functions that make Excel ideal for modeling. You will also learn how to combine functions and where to get help with constructing your formulas where necessary.

Chapter 4, *Applying the Referencing Framework in Excel*, shows you what makes Excel come alive. The referencing framework is what makes Excel dynamic and enables the creation of integrated financial models. A sound knowledge of referencing in Excel can significantly speed up your work and is priceless for reducing the amount of boring repetition. You will learn in an uncomplicated manner how to use relative, absolute, and mixed referencing.

Chapter 5, *Understanding Project and Building Assumptions*, shows the measure of the importance of this topic, because about 75% of your modeling time should be spent on getting to know and understanding the project. As mentioned a number of times, there are different types of model. Which model you use will depend on the nature and purpose of your project, as well as your target audience. When building your assumptions, you will need to interview all those in a position to give informed and accurate growth projections for the various aspects of the entity's operations.

Chapter 6, *Asset and Debt Schedules*, shows us how to prepare an asset schedule to incorporate additions and disposals and current depreciation charges. You will also prepare a debt schedule to reflect projected additional finance and debt repayments as well as interest charges.

Chapter 7, *Cash Flow Statement*, covers the cash flow statement and explains how it is used in financial modeling. We will learn how to generate this as efficiently as possible.

Chapter 8, *Ratio Analysis*, teaches you how to compute performance indicators to give an idea of the projected financial health of the company. You can then compare this with historical ratios and determine whether this is consistent with your projections. The ratios will be divided into the following categories: liquidity, profitability, returns, and gearing.

Chapter 9, *Valuation*, shows us the various types of valuation methods and their advantages and affinity to different models. We will learn about the most accurate method, which is the discounted cash flow method.

`Chapter 10`, *Model Testing for Reasonableness and Accuracy*, provides a way to consider a range of alternatives to some of our key assumptions. Since we have been careful to format our input cells differently, we can quickly identify those inputs that have a significant impact on our final result, change them, and see the effect this has on our valuation. Finally, we look at the presentation of our results with the help of charts.

To get the most out of this book

A basic knowledge of statistics and Excel will be useful, along with a keen interest in financial modeling.

Download the example code files

You can download the example code files for this book from your account at `www.packt.com`. If you purchased this book elsewhere, you can visit `www.packt.com/support` and register to have the files emailed directly to you.

You can download the code files by following these steps:

1. Log in or register at `www.packt.com`.
2. Select the **SUPPORT** tab.
3. Click on **Code Downloads & Errata**.
4. Enter the name of the book in the **Search** box and follow the onscreen instructions.

Once the file is downloaded, please make sure that you unzip or extract the folder using the latest version of:

- WinRAR/7-Zip for Windows
- Zipeg/iZip/UnRarX for Mac
- 7-Zip/PeaZip for Linux

The code bundle for the book is also hosted on GitHub at `https://github.com/PacktPublishing/Hands-On-Financial-Modeling-with-Microsoft-Excel-2019`. In case there's an update to the code, it will be updated on the existing GitHub repository.

We also have other code bundles from our rich catalog of books and videos available at `https://github.com/PacktPublishing/`. Check them out!

Download the color images

We also provide a PDF file that has color images of the screenshots/diagrams used in this book. You can download it here: https://static.packt-cdn.com/downloads/9781789534627_ColorImages.pdf.

Conventions used

There are a number of text conventions used throughout this book.

CodeInText: Indicates code words in text, database table names, folder names, filenames, file extensions, pathnames, dummy URLs, user input, and Twitter handles. Here is an example: "By typing =D4 in cell **F5**, the contents of cell **D4**, Happy day, have been duplicated in cell **F5**."

A block of code is set as follows:

```
=PMT($C$2/$C$4,$C$3*$C$4,$C$5)
```

Bold: Indicates a new term, an important word, or words that you see on screen. For example, words in menus or dialog boxes appear in the text like this. Here is an example: "The rows are labeled **1**, **2**, **3**, and so on, up to **1,048,576**, and the columns are labeled **A**, **B**, **C**, and so on, up to **XFD**."

Warnings or important notes appear like this.

Tips and tricks appear like this.

Get in touch

Feedback from our readers is always welcome.

General feedback: If you have questions about any aspect of this book, mention the book title in the subject of your message and email us at customercare@packtpub.com.

Errata: Although we have taken every care to ensure the accuracy of our content, mistakes do happen. If you have found a mistake in this book, we would be grateful if you would report this to us. Please visit www.packt.com/submit-errata, selecting your book, clicking on the Errata Submission Form link, and entering the details.

Piracy: If you come across any illegal copies of our works in any form on the internet, we would be grateful if you would provide us with the location address or website name. Please contact us at copyright@packt.com with a link to the material.

If you are interested in becoming an author: If there is a topic that you have expertise in, and you are interested in either writing or contributing to a book, please visit authors.packtpub.com.

Reviews

Please leave a review. Once you have read and used this book, why not leave a review on the site that you purchased it from? Potential readers can then see and use your unbiased opinion to make purchase decisions, we at Packt can understand what you think about our products, and our authors can see your feedback on their book. Thank you!

For more information about Packt, please visit packt.com.

Section 1: Financial Modeling - Overview

In this section, you will understand the meaning of financial modeling with Excel, including an overview of the broad steps to follow in building an integrated financial model.

This section comprises the following chapters:

- Chapter 1, *Introduction to Financial Modeling and Excel*
- Chapter 2, *Steps for Building a Financial Model*

1
Introduction to Financial Modeling and Excel

If you asked five professionals the meaning of financial modeling, you would probably get five different answers. The truth is that they would all be correct in their own context. This is inevitable since the boundaries for the use of financial modeling continue to be stretched almost daily, and new users want to define the discipline from their own perspective. In this chapter, you will learn the basic ingredients of a financial model and what my favorite definitions are. You will also learn about the different tools for financial modeling that currently exist in the industry, as well as those features of Excel that make it the ideal tool to use in order to handle the various needs of a financial model.

In this chapter, we will cover the following topics:

- The main ingredients of a financial model
- Understanding mathematical models
- Definitions of financial models
- Types of financial models
- Alternative tools for financial modeling
- Excel—the ideal tool

The main ingredients of a financial model

First of all, there needs to be a situation or problem that requires you to make a financial decision. Your decision will depend on the outcome of two or more options. Let's look at the various aspects of a financial model:

Financial decisions: Financial decisions can be divided into three main types:

- Investment
- Financing
- Distributions or dividends

Investment

We will now look at some reasons for investment decisions:

1. **Purchasing new equipment**: You may already have the capacity and know how to make or build in-house. There may also be similar equipment already in place. Considerations will thus be whether to make or buy, sell, keep, or trade-in the existing equipment.
2. **Business expansion decisions**: This could mean taking on new products, opening up a new branch or expanding an existing branch. The considerations would be to compare the following:

   - **The cost of the investment**: Isolates all costs specific to the investment, for example, construction, additional manpower, added running costs, adverse effect on existing business, marketing costs, and so on.
   - **The benefit gained from the investment**: We can gain additional sales. There will be a boost in other sales as a result of the new investment, along with other quantifiable benefits. To get the **return on investment** (**ROI**), a positive ROI would indicate that the investment is a good one.

Financing decisions primarily revolve around whether to obtain finance from personal funds or from external sources.

For example, if you decided to get a loan to purchase a car, you would need to decide how much you wanted to put down as your contribution, so that the bank would make up the difference. The considerations would be as follows:

- **Interest rates**: The higher the interest rate, the lower the amount you would seek to finance externally
- **Tenor of loan**: The longer the tenor the lower the monthly repayments, but the longer you remain indebted to the bank
- **How much you can afford to contribute**: This will put a platform on the least amount you will require from the bank, no matter what interest rate they are offering
- **Number of monthly repayments**: How much you will be required to pay monthly as a result of the foregoing inputs

Financing

A company would need to decide whether to seek finance from internal sources (approach shareholders for additional equity) or external sources (obtain bank facility). We can see the considerations in the following list:

- **Cost of finance**: The cost of bank finance can be easily obtained as the interest and related charges. These finance charges will have to be paid whether or not the company is making profit. Equity finance is cheaper since the company does not have to pay dividends every year, also the amount paid is at the discretion of the directors.
- **Availability of finance**: It's generally difficult to squeeze more money out of shareholders, unless perhaps there has been a run of good results and decent dividends. So, the company may have no other choice than external finance.
- **The risk inherent in the source**: With external finance there is always the risk that the company may find itself unable to meet the repayments as they are due.
- **The desired debt or equity ratio**: The management of a company will want to maintain a debt to equity ratio that is commensurate with their risk appetite. Risk takers will be comfortable with a ratio of more than 1:1, while risk averse management would prefer a ratio of 1:1 or less.

Dividends

Distributions or dividend decisions are made when there are surplus funds. The decision would be whether to distribute all the surplus, part of the surplus, or none at all. We can see the considerations in the following list:

- **Expectation of the shareholders**: Shareholders provide the cheap finance options and are generally patient. However, they want to be assured that their investment is worthwhile. This is generally manifested by profits, growth, and in particular, dividends, which have an immediate effect on their finances.
- **The need to retain surplus for future growth**: It is the duty of the directors to temper the urge to satisfy the pressure to declare as much dividend as possible, with the necessity to retain at least part of the surplus for future growth and contingencies.
- **The desire to maintain a good dividend policy**: A good dividend policy is necessary to retain the confidence of existing shareholders and to attract potential future investors.

Understanding mathematical models

In the scheme of things, the best or optimum solution is usually measured in monetary terms. This could be the option that generates the highest returns, the least cost option, the option that carries an acceptable level of risk, and the most environmentally friendly option, but is usually a mixture of all these features. Inevitably, there is an inherent uncertainty in the situation, which makes it necessary to make assumptions based on past results. The most appropriate way to capture all the variables inherent in the situation or problem is to create a mathematical model. The model will establish relationships between the variables and assumptions, which serve as an input to the model. This model will include a series of calculations to evaluate the input information and to clarify and present the various alternatives and their consequences. It is this model that is referred to as a financial model.

Definitions of financial models

Wikipedia considers a financial model to be a mathematical model that represents the performance of a financial asset, project, or other investments in abstract form.

Corporate Finance Institute believes that a financial model facilitates the forecasting of future financial performance, by utilizing certain variables to estimate the outcome of specific financial decisions.

Business Dictionary agrees with the notion of a mathematical model in that it comprises sets of equations. The model analyzes how an entity will react to different economic situations with a focus on the outcome of financial decisions. It goes on to list some of the statements and schedules you would expect to find in a financial model. Additionally, the publication considers that a model could estimate the financial impact of a company's policies and restrictions put in place by investors and lenders. It goes on to give the example of a cash budget as a simple financial model.

eFinance Management considers a financial model to be a tool with which the financial analyst attempts to predict the earnings and performance of future years. It considers the completed model to be a mathematical representation of business transactions. The publication names Excel as the primary tool for modeling.

Here's my personal definition:

> *"A financial decision making a situation prompts the creation of a mathematical model to facilitate the decision making. Preferred courses of action and their consequences are based on the results of the calculations performed by the model."*

Types of financial models

There are several different types of financial models. The model type depends on the purpose and the audience of the model. Generally speaking, you can create a financial model when you want to value or to project something or have a mixture of the two.

The following models are examples that seek to calculate values.

The 3 statement model

In the following screenshot, we see the starting point for most valuation models and what it includes:

Wazobia Global Limited

Balance Check		TRUE	TRUE	TRUE	TRUE	TRUE	TRUE	TRUE	TRUE
(Unless otherwise specified, all financials are in N '000	Units	Y01A	Y02A	Y03A	Y04A	Y05A	Y06F	Y07F	Y08F
ASSUMPTIONS									
BALANCE SHEET									
ASSETS									
Non current assets									
Property, plant and equipment		90,000	80,000	70,000	240,000	210,000	180,000	150,000	120,000
Investments		12,197	11,549	58,106	63,106	58,106	58,106	58,106	58,106
Total non current assets		102,197	91,549	128,106	303,106	268,106	238,106	208,106	178,106
Current assets									
Inventories		15,545	18,007	21,731	14,530	14,530	20,274	14,778	20,525
Trade and other receivables		20,864	31,568	35,901	28,054	28,054	39,026	31,097	42,207
Cash and cash equivalents		7,459	17,252	9,265	110,863	148,306	178,435	243,864	290,573
Total current assets		43,868	66,827	66,897	153,447	190,890	237,736	289,739	353,305
Current liabilities									
Trade and other payables		12,530	16,054	15,831	14,072	14,072	15,682	14,285	15,896
Overdraft		-	-	-	-	-	-	-	-
Total current liabilites		12,530	16,054	15,831	14,072	14,072	15,682	14,285	15,896
Net current assets		31,338	50,773	51,066	139,375	176,818	222,054	275,454	337,409
Total Assets less current liabilities		133,535	142,322	179,172	442,481	444,924	460,160	483,560	515,515
Non current liabilities									
Unsecured loans		40,000	35,000	30,000	275,000	270,000	265,000	260,000	255,000
Other non current liabilities		5,000	5,000	5,000	10,000	5,000	5,000	5,000	5,000
Total non current liabilities		45,000	40,000	35,000	285,000	275,000	270,000	265,000	260,000
Equity									
Share capital		70,000	70,000	70,000	70,000	70,000	70,000	70,000	70,000
Retained earnings		18,535	32,322	74,172	87,481	99,924	120,160	148,560	185,515
Total equity		88,535	102,322	144,172	157,481	169,924	190,160	218,560	255,515
Total equity and non current liabilities		133,535	142,322	179,172	442,481	444,924	460,160	483,560	515,515

1. **Balance sheet (or statement of financial position)**: This is a statement of assets (which are resources owned by the company that have economic value, and that are usually used to generate income for the company, such as plant, machinery, and inventory), liabilities (which are obligations of the company, such as accounts payable and bank loans) and owner's equity (which is a measure of the owner's investment in the company):

A B	C	D	E	F	G	H	I	J	K	L
Balance Check			TRUE	TRUE	TRUE	TRUE	TRUE	TRUE	TRUE	TRUE
(Unless otherwise specified, all financials are in N '000)	Units		Y01A	Y02A	Y03A	Y04A	Y05A	Y06F	Y07F	Y08F
PROFIT & LOSS										
Revenue			260,810	272,241	285,009	297,938	311,453	325,582	340,351	355,791
Cost of sales			177,782	184,703	179,052	179,690	180,331	181,619	182,917	184,223
GROSS PROFIT			83,028	87,538	105,957	118,247	131,122	143,962	157,434	171,567
Sales and marketing expenses			9,204	10,521	11,099	11,210	11,719	12,250	12,806	13,387
General and administration expenses			25,145	26,402	21,752	26,786	28,001	29,271	30,599	31,987
Depreciation			10,000	10,000	10,000	30,000	30,000	30,000	30,000	30,000
Other expenses			5,675	13,342	4,394	8,559	8,948	9,353	9,778	10,221
OPERATING PROFIT			33,004	27,273	58,712	41,692	52,455	63,088	74,252	85,972
Other income			3,333	2,183	2,156	2,156	2,156	2,156	2,156	2,156
Other Finance cost			9,265	9,644	9,848	9,586	9,586	9,586	9,586	9,586
EBIT			25,072	16,062	47,770	19,013	17,775	28,908	40,572	52,792
Interest			2,000	3,750	3,250	15,250	27,250	26,750	26,250	25,750
PROFIT BEFORE TAX			23,072	12,312	44,520	3,763	(9,475)	2,158	14,322	27,042
Income tax expense			6,537	2,275	5,920	5,704	5,333	8,672	12,172	15,838
PROFIT AFTER TAX			18,535	13,787	41,850	13,309	12,443	20,236	28,401	36,955

2. **Income statement (or statement of comprehensive income)**: This is a statement that summarizes the performance of a company by comparing the income it has generated within a specified period to the expenses it has incurred over the same period:

Wazobia Global Limited

Balance Check		TRUE	TRUE	TRUE	TRUE	TRUE	TRUE	TRUE	TRUE
(Unless otherwise specified,	Units	Y01A	Y02A	Y03A	Y04A	Y05A	Y06F	Y07F	Y08F
CASH FLOW STATEMENT									
Cashflow from Operating Activities									
PAT		13,787	41,850	13,309	12,443	20,236	28,401	36,955
Add: Depreciation		10,000	10,000	30,000	30,000	30,000	30,000	30,000
Add: Interest Expense		3,750	3,250	15,250	27,250	26,750	26,250	25,750
Net Change in Working Capital									
Add: Increase in Accounts payable		3,524	(223)	(1,759)	-	1,610	(1,397)	1,611
Less: Increase in Inventory		(2,462)	(3,724)	7,201	0	(5,745)	5,496	(5,747)
Less: Increase in Account Receivables		(10,704)	(4,333)	7,847	-	(10,972)	7,929	(11,110)
Net Change in Working Capital		(9,642)	(8,280)	13,290	0	(15,107)	12,028	(15,245)
Cashflow from Operations		17,895	46,820	71,849	69,693	61,879	96,678	77,460
Cashflow from Investment Activities									
Less: Capex		-	-	(2,00,000)	-	-	-	-
Add: Proceeds from Disposal of Assets					-	-	-	-
Less: Increase in WIP					-	-	-	
Less: Increase in Investments		648	(46,557)	(5,000)	5,000	-	-	-
Cashflow from Investment Activities		648	(46,557)	(2,05,000)	5,000	-	-	-
Cashflow from Financing Activities									
Add: New Equity Raised								
Add: New Unsecured Loans Raised		-	-	2,50,000				-
Less: Unsecured Loans Repaid		(5,000)	(5,000)	(5,000)	(5,000)	(5,000)	(5,000)	(5,000)
Less: Dividends Paid								
Less: Interest Expense		(3,750)	(3,250)	(15,250)	(27,250)	(26,750)	(26,250)	(25,750)
Cashflow from Financing Activities		(8,750)	(8,250)	2,29,750	(32,250)	(31,750)	(31,250)	(30,750)
Net Cashflow		9,793	(7,987)	96,599	42,443	30,129	65,428	46,710
Cash Balance								
Opening Balance		7,459	17,252	9,265	1,05,864	1,48,306	1,78,435	2,43,864
Net Cashflow		9,793	(7,987)	96,599	42,443	30,129	65,428	46,710
Closing Balance		17,252	9,265	1,05,864	1,48,306	1,78,435	2,43,864	2,90,573

3. **Cash flow statement:** This is a statement that identifies inflow and outflow of cash to and from various sources, operations, and transactions, during the period under review. The net cash inflow should equal the movement in cash and cash equivalents shown in the balance sheet during the period under review.

The mathematics of this model starts with historical data. In other words, the income statement, the balance sheet, and the cash flow statement for the previous 3 to 5 years will be entered into Excel. A set of assumptions will be made and used to drive the financial results as displayed in the three statements, over the next 3 to 5 years. This will be illustrated more in detail later in the book and will become clearer. The following screenshot shows an example of a cash flow statement:

		Y01A	Y02A	Y03A	Y04F	Y05F	Y06F	Y07F	Y08F
3									
4	Balance Check	TRUE	TRUE	TRUE	TRUE	TRUE	TRUE	TRUE	TRUE
5									
6	(Unless otherwise specified, all financials an Units	Y01A	Y02A	Y03A	Y04F	Y05F	Y06F	Y07F	Y08F
113	**CASH FLOW STATEMENT**								
114									
115	**Cashflow from Operating Activities**								
116	PAT		13,787	1,850	13,309	13,318	23,312	33,684	44,449
117	Add: Depreciation		10,000	10,000	30,000	30,000	30,000	30,000	30,000
118	Add: Interest Expense		3,750	3,250	15,250	26,000	23,000	20,000	17,000
119									
120	**Net Change in Working Capital**								
121	Add: Increase in Accounts payable		3,524	(223)	(1,759)	1,865	(1,758)	1,866	(1,758)
122	Less: Increase in Inventory		(2,462)	(3,724)	7,201	(7,331)	7,201	(7,331)	7,201
123	Less: Increase in Account Receivables		(10,704)	(4,333)	2,089	(5,252)	1,946	(5,402)	1,789
124	Net Change in Working Capital		(9,642)	(8,280)	7,532	(10,717)	7,389	(10,867)	7,232
125									
126	**Cashflow from Operations**		17,895	6,820	66,091	58,600	83,701	72,816	98,681
127									
128	**Cashflow from Investment Activities**								
129	Less: Capex		-	-	(200,000)	-	-	-	-
130	Add: Proceeds from Disposal of Assets								
131	Less: Increase in WIP								
132	Less: Increase in Investments		648	(6,557)	(40,000)	-	-	-	-
133	Cashflow from Investment Activities		648	(6,557)	(240,000)	-	-	-	-
134									
135	**Cashflow from Financing Activities**								
136	Add: New Equity Raised								
137	Add: New Unsecured Loans Raised		-	-	250,000	-	-	-	-
138	Less: Unsecured Loans Repaid		(5,000)	(5,000)	(5,000)	(30,000)	(30,000)	(30,000)	(30,000)
139	Less: Dividends Paid								
140	Less: Interest Expense		(3,750)	(3,250)	(15,250)	(26,000)	(23,000)	(20,000)	(17,000)
141	Cashflow from Financing Activities		(8,750)	(8,250)	229,750	(56,000)	(53,000)	(50,000)	(47,000)
142									
143	**Net Cashflow**		9,793	(7,987)	55,841	2,600	30,701	22,816	51,681
144									
145	**Cash Balance**								
146	Opening Balance		7,459	17,252	9,265	65,106	67,707	98,408	121,224
147	Net Cashflow		9,793	(7,987)	55,841	2,600	30,701	22,816	51,681
148	Closing Balance		17,252	9,265	65,106	67,707	98,408	121,224	172,905

The discounted cash flow model

The **discounted cash flow** (**DCF**) method is considered by most experts to be the most accurate for valuing a company. Essentially, the method considers the value of a company to be the sum of all the future cash flows the company can generate. In reality the cash is adjusted for various obligations to arrive at the free cash flow. The method also considers the time value of money, a concept with which we will become much more familiar in a later chapter. The DCF method applies a valuation model to the 3 statement model mentioned in *The 3 statement model* section. Later, we will encounter and explain fully the technical parameters included in this valuation model.

The comparative companies model

This method relies on the theory that similar companies will have similar multiples. Multiples are, for example, comparing the value of the company or enterprise (**enterprise value** or **EV**) to its earnings. There are different levels of earnings, such as the following:

- **Earnings before interest, tax, depreciation, and amortization (EBITDA)**
- **Earnings before interest and tax (EBIT)**
- **Profit before tax (PBT)**
- **Profit after tax (PAT)**

For each of them, a number of multiples can be generated and used to arrive at a range of EVs for the company. The comparative method is simplistic and highly subjective especially in the choice of comparable companies; however, it is favored amongst analysts, as it provides a quick way of arriving at an indication of the value for a company.

Again, this method relies on the 3 statement model as a starting point. You then identify three to five similar companies with the quoted EVs. In selecting similar companies (**peer group**), the criteria to consider will include the nature of the business, size in terms of assets and/or turnover, geographical location, and more. We use the following steps to do so:

1. We need to calculate the multiples for each of the companies (such as *EV/EBITDA, EV/SALES, P/E* ratio).
2. Then calculate the mean and median of the multiples of all the similar companies.

The median is often preferred over the mean, as it corrects the effect of the outliers. Outliers are those individual items within a sample that are significantly larger or smaller than the other items, and thus tend to skew the mean one way or the other.

3. Then adopt the median multiplier for your target company and substitute the earnings, for example, EBITDA, calculated in the 3 statement model in the equation:

$$Multiple = EV/EBITDA$$

4. When you rearrange the formula, you arrive at the EV for the target company:

$$EV = Multiple \times EBITDA$$

The merger and acquisition model

When two companies seek to merge, or one seeks to acquire the other, investment analysts build a **mergers and acquisitions (M&A)** model. Valuation models are first built for the individual companies separately then a model is built for the combined post-merger entity and their earnings per share calculated. The **earnings per share (EPS)** is an indicator of a company's profitability. It is calculated as net income divided by number of shares. The purpose of the model is to determine the effect of the merger on the acquiring company's EPS. If there is an increase in post-merger EPS then the merger is accretive, otherwise it is dilutive.

The leveraged buyout model

In a leveraged buyout situation, company A acquires company B for a combination of cash (equity) and loan (debt). The debt portion tends to be significant. Company A then runs company B, servicing the debt, and then sells company B after 3 to 5 years. The **leveraged buyout model (LBO)** model will calculate a value for company B as well as the likely return on the eventual sale of the company.

We will now look at models that project something.

Loan repayment schedule

When you approach your bank for a car loan, your accounts officer takes you through the structure of the loan including loan amount, interest rate, monthly repayments, and sometimes, how much you can afford to contribute towards the cost of the car. Let us look at the various features of loans in the following screenshot:

Amortization Table

Assumptions	
Cost of Asset	20,000,000
Customer's Contribn	10%
Loan Amount	18,000,000
Interest Rate (Annual)	10%
Tenor (Years)	10
Payment periods per year	12
Interest Rate (Periodic)	0.83%
Total periods	120
Periodic Repayment (PMT)	=-PMT(C11,C12,C7)

Periods	PMT	Interest Paid	Principal Reduction	Balance
0				18,000,000.00
1	237,871.33	150,000.00	87,871.33	17,912,128.67
2	237,871.33	149,267.74	88,603.59	17,823,525.09
3	237,871.33	148,529.38	89,341.95	17,734,183.14
4	237,871.33	147,784.86	90,086.47	17,644,096.67
5	237,871.33	147,034.14	90,837.19	17,553,259.48
6	237,871.33	146,277.16	91,594.16	17,461,665.32
7	237,871.33	145,513.88	92,357.45	17,369,307.87
8	237,871.33	144,744.23	93,127.09	17,276,180.77
9	237,871.33	143,968.17	93,903.15	17,182,277.62
10	237,871.33	143,185.65	94,685.68	17,087,591.94
11	237,871.33	142,396.60	95,474.73	16,992,117.21
12	237,871.33	141,600.98	96,270.35	16,895,846.86
13	237,871.33	140,798.72	97,072.60	16,798,774.26
14	237,871.33	139,989.79	97,881.54	16,700,892.72
15	237,871.33	139,174.11	98,697.22	16,602,195.50
16	237,871.33	138,351.63	99,519.70	16,502,675.80
17	237,871.33	137,522.30	100,349.03	16,402,326.78
18	237,871.33	136,686.06	101,185.27	16,301,141.51
19	237,871.33	135,842.85	102,028.48	16,199,113.03
20	237,871.33	134,992.61	102,878.72	16,096,234.31
21	237,871.33	134,135.29	103,736.04	15,992,498.27
22	237,871.33	133,270.82	104,600.51	15,887,897.76
23	237,871.33	132,399.15	105,472.18	15,782,425.58
24	237,871.33	131,520.21	106,351.11	15,676,074.47
25	237,871.33	130,633.95	107,237.37	15,568,837.10
26	237,871.33	129,740.31	108,131.02	15,460,706.08
27	237,871.33	128,839.22	109,032.11	15,351,673.97
28	237,871.33	127,930.62	109,940.71	15,241,733.26

The preceding screenshot gives us an example of how you would lay out your assumptions for a loan repayment schedule model. The monthly repayment is calculated using Excel's PMT function. The tenure is 10 years, but repayment is monthly (12 repayment periods per year), giving a total number of periods of *(nper)() of 12 × 10 = 120*. Note that the annual interest rate will have to be converted to a rate per period, which is 10%/12 (rate/periods), to give 0.83% per month in our example. The pv is the loan amount. We also need to keep in mind that the actual loan amount is the cost of the asset less customer's contribution.

Selection scroll bars have been added to the model so that customer's contribution (10%-25%), interest rate (18%-21%), and tenor (5–10 years) can be easily varied and the results immediately observed since the parameters will recalculate at once.

The preceding screenshot shows the kind of amortization table they use in order to turn around your options so quickly.

The budget model

A **budget model** is a financial plan of cash inflows and outflows of a company. It builds scenarios of required or standard results, for turnover, purchases, assets, debt, and more. It can then compare the actual with the budget or forecast and make decisions based on the results. Budget models are typically monthly or quarterly and focus heavily on the profit and loss account. Other types of financial models include the following:

- Initial public offer model
- Sum of the parts model
- Consolidation model
- Options pricing model

Alternative tools for financial modeling

Excel has always been recognized as the go-to software for financial modeling. However, there are significant shortcomings in Excel that have made the serious modeler look for alternatives, in particular in the case of complex models. The following aspects are some of the disadvantages of Excel that financial modeling software seeks to correct:

- **Large datasets**: Excel struggles with very large data. After most actions, Excel recalculates all formulas included in your model. For most users, this happens so quickly that you don't even notice. However, with large amounts of data and complex formulas, delays in recalculation become quite noticeable, and can be very frustrating. Alternative software can handle huge multidimensional datasets that include complex formulas.

- **Data extraction**: In the course of your modeling, you will need to extract data from the internet and other sources. For example, financial statements from a company's website, exchange rates from multiple sources, and more. This data comes in different formats with varying degrees of structure. Excel does a relatively good job of extracting data from these sources. However, it has to be done manually, and thus it is tedious and limited by the skill set of the user. Oracle BI, Tableau, and SAS are built, among other things, to automate the extraction and analysis of data.

- **Risk management**: A very important part of financial analysis is **risk management**. Let's look at some examples of risk management here:
  - **Human error**: Here, we talk about the risk associated with the consequences of human error. With Excel, exposure to human error is significant and unavoidable. Most alternative modeling software is built with error prevention as a prime consideration. As many of the procedures are automated, this reduces the possibility of human error to a bare minimum.

- **Error in assumptions**: When building your model, you need to make a number of assumptions since you are making an educated guess as to what might happen in the future. As essential as these assumptions are, they are necessarily subjective. Different modelers faced with the same set of circumstances may come up with different sets of assumptions leading to quite different outcomes. This is why it is always necessary to test the accuracy of your model by substituting a range of alternative values for key assumptions and observe how this affects the model. This procedure, referred to as sensitivity and scenario analyses, is an essential part of modeling. These analyses can be done in Excel, but they are always limited in scope and are done manually. Alternative software can easily utilize the Monte Carlo simulation for different variables or sets of variables to supply a range of likely results as well as the probability that they will occur. The Monte Carlo simulation is a mathematical technique that substitutes a range of values for various assumptions, and then runs calculations over and over again. The procedure can involve tens of thousands of calculations until it eventually produces a distribution of possible outcomes. The distribution indicates the chance or probability of individual results happening.

Advantages of Excel

In spite of all the shortcomings of Excel, and the very impressive results from alternative modeling software, Excel continues to be the preferred tool for financial modeling.

Let us take a deeper look at the advantages of Excel in the following section:

- **Already on your computer**: You probably already have Excel installed on your computer. The alternative modeling software tends to be proprietary and has to be installed on your computer manually.
- **Familiar software**: About 80% of users already have a working knowledge of Excel. The alternative modeling software will usually have a significant learning curve in order to get used to unfamiliar procedures.
- **No extra cost**: You will most likely already have a subscription to Microsoft Office including Excel. The cost of installing new specialized software and teaching potential users how to use the software tends to be high and continuous. Each new batch of users has to undergo training on the alternative software at additional cost.

- **Flexibility**: The alternative modeling software is usually built to handle certain specific sets of conditions, so that while they are structured and accurate under those specific circumstances, they are rigid and cannot be modified to handle cases that differ significantly from the default conditions. Excel is flexible and can be adapted to different purposes.
- **Portability**: Models prepared with the alternative software cannot be readily shared with other users, or outside of an organization since the other party must have the same software in order to make sense of the model. Excel is the same from user to user right across geographical boundaries.
- **Compatibility**: Excel communicates very well with other software. Almost all software can produce output, in one form or the other, that can be understood by Excel. Similarly, Excel can produce output in formats that many different software can read. In other words, there is compatibility whether you wish to import or export data.
- **Superior learning experience**: Building a model from scratch with Excel gives the user a great learning experience. You gain a better understanding of the project and of the entity being modeled. You also learn the connection and relationship between different parts of the model.

Excel – the ideal tool

The following features make Excel the ideal tool for any data:

- **Understanding data**: No other software mimics human understanding the way Excel does. Excel understands that there are 60 seconds in a minute, 60 minutes in an hour, 24 hours in a day, and so on to weeks, months and years. Excel knows the days of the week, months of the year, and their abbreviations, for example, Wed for Wednesday, Aug for August, and 03 for March! Excel even knows which months have 30 days, which months have 31 days, which years have 28 days in February, and which are leap years and have 29 days. It can differentiate between numbers and text, it also knows that you can add, subtract, multiply, and divide numbers, and we can arrange text in alphabetical order. On the foundation of this human-like understanding of these parameters, Excel has built an amazing array of features and functions that allow the user to extract almost unimaginable detail from an array of data.

- **Navigation**: Models can very quickly become very large, and with Excel's capacity, most models will be limited only by your imagination and appetite. This can make your model unwieldy and difficult to navigate. Excel is wealthy in navigation tools and shortcuts, it makes the process less stressful and even enjoyable. The following are examples of some of the navigation tools:

  - *Ctrl + PgUp/PgDn*: These keys allow you to quickly move from one worksheet to the next. *Ctrl + PgDn* jumps to the next worksheet and *Ctrl + PgUp* jumps to the previous worksheet.
  - *Ctrl + Arrow Key* ($\rightarrow\downarrow\leftarrow\uparrow$): If the active cell (the cell you're in) is blank, then pressing *Ctrl + Arrow key* will cause the cursor to jump to the first populated cell in the direction of the cursor. If the active cell is populated, then pressing *Ctrl + Arrow key* will cause the cursor to jump to the last populated cell before a blank cell, in the direction of the cursor.

Summary

In this chapter, we looked at the main ingredients that make up a financial model. We looked at various types of financial models and how they work in Excel. We also looked at alternative tools for financial modeling and the various advantages that Excel has. Finally, we saw all the various reasons why Excel is the ideal tool for creating financial models.

In the next chapter, we will see the various steps involved in creating a model.

2
Steps for Building a Financial Model

Any project you wish to undertake should begin with gaining an accurate understanding of what the project is all about. If you start off in the wrong direction, one of three things will happen:

- Part way through the project, you'll realize that this is not what the client wants, and you'll then have to start all over again
- You'll end up convincing the client to accept a project that was never intended
- You'll persist with the wrong project and it'll end up being rejected

So much depends on this stage that it typically takes up about 75% of your total modeling time.

In this chapter, we will cover the following topics:

- Discussions with management
- Building assumptions
- Building a template for your model
- Historical data
- Projecting the balance sheet and profit and loss account
- Additional schedules and projections
- Cash flow statement
- Valuation

Discussions with management

This is where you determine or confirm the scope and target of your model. Management is also the primary source of information about future plans and trends.

Usually, it's not possible to get all of the details at the first time of asking. You should, therefore, be prepared to go back to the section heads and ask the same or similar questions from a position of better understanding.

Gauging management expectations

While discussing with management, you need to get a clear understanding of their expectations from the assignment and what they hope will be achieved.

If all that is required is a projected cash flow, then a full-blown valuation model would be a waste of time and resources and you probably wouldn't get paid for the extra work. We will take a detailed look at the all-important cash flow statement and different valuation models later in this book.

Knowing your client's business

It is essential that you know the client's business thoroughly. You need to know the industry of the business and identify any peculiarities due to geographical location, as well as those specific to the client. You should also gain some knowledge of the trends in the industry, and who the client's competitors are. If the client operates in a specialized industry, you need to consider consulting with someone who is an expert in that field. Whenever there is uncertainty, corroborative evidence is one of the best forms of assurance that you are doing the right thing.

Department heads

It is the department heads that will contribute the most toward building assumptions about future growth and expected trends. They have been in their respective areas of expertise for years and have come to understand the business better than most. As a result, you should place reliance on their responses.

You should therefore be in a position to assess how competent they are to give credible insight to the company's plans.

Building assumptions

Financial modeling is all about projecting results or behavior into the future.

To do this, you will need to build up a set of assumptions to bridge the gap between actual performance and future results. Although you will need to project every single item in the model, your assumptions will focus on items that will have a material effect on the final results. Other non-material items can be projected as, say, percentage of turnover (for revenue items) or a best judgement figure (for balance sheet items).

Your assumptions will need to consider whether items will increase, decrease, or stay the same. How you calculate the projected change is referred to as the growth driver. For example, for revenue items, it could be inflation, year-on-year growth, or some other indicator.

Building a template for your model

It is always important to be systematic in the way you build and maintain your model. Even if you alone will make use of the model, whenever you have cause to revisit the model after a period of time, you would not want to have to wade through various schedules and worksheets to find what you need.

This is even more important if your model is going to be used by someone else.

A good way to ensure that your model is easy to follow, and use is to build a template (a standard format) with some simple rules guiding how data is to be input and presented. In general, you will require at least six columns of figures, three each of historical and projected years, and another three or four columns for descriptive information. The template should enhance navigation and be easy to follow. The first major decision is whether to adopt a single worksheet or multiple worksheet approach.

The following are some of the pros and cons of both approaches:

- **Multiple worksheet approach**: In a multiple worksheet approach, each worksheet is dedicated to one statement. So, you have assumptions, balance sheet, profit and loss, cash flow statements, and so on, all on separate worksheets. This means that you will end up with 10 or more worksheets. The following screenshot gives an indication of the multiple tabs required in this approach:

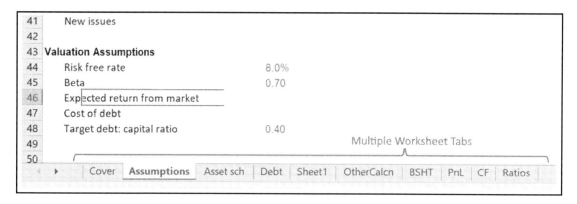

When you dedicate one worksheet to one statement only, for example, the balance sheet, you know that everything on the balance sheet worksheet relates to the balance sheet alone. There is no ambiguous content on the worksheet. If you then need to modify or query the content of that worksheet, you can do so without having to consider whether or not you are affecting a statement other than the balance sheet.

In order to facilitate efficient navigation through your model, you should ensure that each year is in the same column on each worksheet. So that, if the Y05F year is in column **J** on the balance sheet worksheet, it should be in column **J** on the profit and loss, cash flow, and all other worksheets.

- **Single worksheet approach**: In order to follow this approach, you must ensure that you maintain a standard layout for all statements right from the outset. Any change to column width or attempts to insert or delete columns will affect all statements since they are stacked one on top of the other. An important part of this approach is the grouping of each statement. Excel allows you to group rows so that they can be collapsed and hidden or expanded and revealed by clicking the – or + that is displayed alongside the row labels when the group is created. The following screenshot is an example of the single worksheet approach:

Wazobia Global Limited

Balance Check		TRUE	TRUE	TRUE	TRUE	TRUE
(Unless otherwise specified, all finar	Units	Y01A	Y02A	Y03A	Y04A	Y05A
Accumulated Depreciation						
Opening Balance		-	10,000	20,000	30,000	60,000
Add: Depreciation during current year		10,000	10,000	10,000	30,000	30,000
Closing Balance		**10,000**	**20,000**	**30,000**	**60,000**	**90,000**
Net Book Value		90,000	80,000	70,000	240,000	210,000

DEBT SCHEDULE

Unsecured Loans						
Opening		-	40,000	35,000	30,000	275,000
Additions		40,000	-	-	250,000	-
Repayments 0n 40M	8 yrs		5,000	5,000	5,000	5,000
Repayments 0n 250M	10 yrs					
Closing	0	40,000	35,000	30,000	275,000	270,000
Interest rate		10%	10%	10%	10%	10%
Interest		2,000	3,750	3,250	15,250	27,250

SOCI - OTHER CALCN

Equity						
Opening		70,000	70,000	70,000	70,000	70,000
Additions		-	-	-	-	-
Closing		70,000	70,000	70,000	70,000	70,000
Retained earnings						
Opening		-	18,535	32,322	74,172	87,481
Result for the year - PAT		18,535	13,787	41,850	13,309	12,443
Closing		18,535	32,322	74,172	87,481	99,924

RATIOS

Profitability Ratios						
EBIT Margin		10%	7%	4%	11%	14%
PBT Margin		10%	6%	3%	6%	6%
PAT Margin		7%	5%	1%	4%	4%

| Cover | Financial Model | Valuation | ⊕ |

There are vertical lines, down the left border, just before the row numbers. The length of each vertical line covers the range of rows included in that particular group. The collapse or expand button is displayed at the end of the line, just after the last row of the group. It appears as a – sign when the group is expanded. Clicking the – sign will collapse the group and turn the sign to a + sign. You click the + sign if you wish to expand the group.

You will create the groups so that, when you collapse a statement, the title of that statement will remain visible as shown in the following screenshot. In this screenshot, you will notice that, with the schedules collapsed, row **8** is followed by row **57**. The rows in between house the ASSUMPTIONS schedule. By pressing the + sign beside the row **57** label, the group will be expanded to expose the full schedule. The following screenshot is an example of how your groups should look when arranged properly:

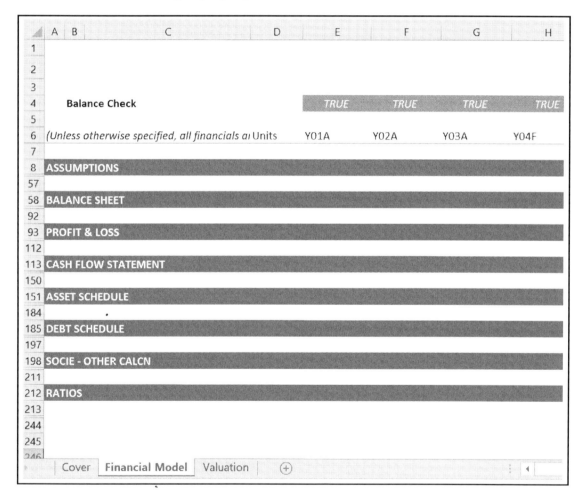

Next, we will look at the column layout. With navigation issues at the back of your mind, reduce the width of the first two columns, **A** and **B**, and expand column **C**, as shown in the following screenshot. Column **A** will be used for the first level of titles, column **B** for the second level of titles, and column **C** the description or details that would require a wider column.

The following screenshot shows how your model template should look:

			Units	Y01A	Y02A	Y03A	Y04F	Y05F
Wazobia Global Limited								
Balance Check				*TRUE*	*TRUE*	*TRUE*	*TRUE*	
(Unless otherwise specified, all financials			Units	Y01A	Y02A	Y03A	Y04F	Y05F
ASSUMPTIONS								
Revenue Assumptions								
	Revenue			260,810	272,241	285,009	297,938	
		Growth %			4%	5%	4.5%	
	Cost of sales			177,782	184,703	179,052	179,690	
		Growth %			4%	-3%	0.4%	
	Sales and marketing expenses			9,204	10,521	11,099	11,210	
		Sales and mktng exps as a % of Revenue		4%	4%	4%	3.8%	
	General and administration expenses			25,145	26,402	21,752	26,786	
		Gen & admin exps as a % of Revenue		10%	10%	8%	9.0%	
	Other expenses			5,675	13,342	4,394	8,559	
		Other exps as a % of Revenue		2%	5%	2%	2.9%	
	Other income			3,333	2,183	2,156	2,156	
Balance Sheet Assumptions								
	Key Ratios							
		Inventories (Days of cost of sales)			33	41	37	

This arrangement gives a cascading effect and facilitates quick navigation between headings of the same level, using Excel keyboard shortcuts. For example, with the cursor on ASSUMPTIONS, cell **A8**, pressing *Ctrl* + the down arrow (↓) will cause the cursor to jump down to cell **A25**, Balance Sheet Assumptions. Column **D** will be for the Units and column **E** for the first year of historical financials. As mentioned earlier in this chapter, the years should retain the same column on every worksheet in the multiple worksheet approach. With the single worksheet approach, this is not an issue as the statements are stacked one on top of another.

- **Color coding**: This is a method used to differentiate between typed-in (hardcoded) cells that may be changed and revised, and those cells that contain formulas. Hardcoded cells should be in blue font with calculated cells retaining the default black color. This will be very helpful when troubleshooting or when there is the need to amend original assumptions. You will be able to very quickly identify the input cells, which are the only cells that may require modifying.
- **Freeze panes**: With this option, you will be able to leave titles and column headings visible when you scroll down below their usual level of visibility. You should freeze panes, so that the balance sheet **Balance Check** and the **Years** will remain visible in the frozen rows.
- **Rounding off**: The significance of rounding off becomes apparent when you have to populate 10 columns with annual financials. Screen space gets filled up very quickly, making it necessary to scroll to the right in order to view some of the data.

As much as possible, you should round off your figures so that all of the years fit within one screen width.

Historical financial data

Once you have the template in place, the next step is to obtain historical financials. With historical data, we are interested in the balance sheet, profit and loss account, and cash flow statement. It is common, in the course of preparing financial statements, to have a number of initial drafts which may have content that will been superseded when the final statements are agreed. Ensure that the financials you are given are the final audited financial statements. The more information you have, the more accurate your projections. However, you must not get carried away, as too much information will make the model unnecessarily cumbersome. Generally, historical data is limited to five years, with another five years of projected financials. Try to get soft copies of the historical financials in Excel readable format, as this will significantly reduce the amount of time you will need to spend converting into your template format.

Inevitably, you will need to tidy up the data to bring formatting and arrangement in line with your model template and other anomalies. The actual figures from the historical financials will not change as you create your model; however, more often than not, you would have obtained the financials from a source that works with different preferences and priorities to yours. Moreover, the financials were not prepared with you and your financial model in mind. Imported data is therefore riddled with formatting or presentation anomalies, which make it difficult and sometimes impossible to utilize some Excel tools and shortcuts. This makes it necessary to retype some or all of the financials.

The following screenshot is the published balance sheet at **August 31, 2016** of **ACCENTURE PLC**, extracted from the Accenture website (`https://www.accenture.com/_acnmedia/PDF-35/Accenture-2016-Shareholder-Letter10-K006.pdf`). It illustrates how even the most accomplished financials will need to be adjusted to suit your template:

ACCENTURE PLC
CONSOLIDATED BALANCE SHEETS
August 31, 2016 and 2015
(In thousands of U.S. dollars, except share and per share amounts)

	August 31, 2016	August 31, 2015
ASSETS		
CURRENT ASSETS:		
Cash and cash equivalents	$ 4,905,609	$ 4,360,766
Short-term investments	2,875	2,448
Receivables from clients, net	4,072,180	3,840,920
Unbilled services, net	2,150,219	1,884,504
Other current assets	845,339	611,436
Total current assets	11,976,222	10,700,074
NON-CURRENT ASSETS:		
Unbilled services, net	68,145	15,501
Investments	198,633	45,027
Property and equipment, net	956,542	801,884
Goodwill	3,609,437	2,929,833
Deferred contract costs	733,219	655,482
Deferred income taxes, net	2,077,312	2,089,928
Other non-current assets	989,494	964,918
Total non-current assets	8,632,782	7,502,573
TOTAL ASSETS	$ 20,609,004	$ 18,202,647
LIABILITIES AND SHAREHOLDERS' EQUITY		
CURRENT LIABILITIES:		
Current portion of long-term debt and bank borrowings	$ 2,773	$ 1,848
Accounts payable	1,280,821	1,151,464
Deferred revenues	2,364,728	2,251,617
Accrued payroll and related benefits	4,040,751	3,687,468
Accrued consumption taxes	358,359	319,350
Income taxes payable	362,963	516,827
Other accrued liabilities	468,529	562,432
Total current liabilities	8,878,924	8,491,006
NON-CURRENT LIABILITIES:		
Long-term debt	24,457	25,587
Deferred revenues	754,812	524,455
Retirement obligation	1,494,789	1,108,623
Deferred income taxes, net	111,020	91,372
Income taxes payable	850,709	996,077
Other non-current liabilities	304,917	317,956
Total non-current liabilities	3,540,704	3,064,070
COMMITMENTS AND CONTINGENCIES		
SHAREHOLDERS' EQUITY:		
Ordinary shares, par value 1.00 euros per share, 40,000 shares authorized and issued as of August 31, 2016 and August 31, 2015	57	57
Class A ordinary shares, par value $0.0000225 per share, 20,000,000,000 shares authorized, 654,202,813 and 804,757,785 shares issued as of August 31, 2016 and August 31, 2015, respectively	15	18
Class X ordinary shares, par value $0.0000225 per share, 1,000,000,000 shares authorized, 21,917,155 and 23,335,142 shares issued and outstanding as of August 31, 2016 and August 31, 2015, respectively	—	1
Restricted share units	1,004,128	1,031,203
Additional paid-in capital	2,924,729	4,516,810
Treasury shares, at cost: Ordinary, 40,000 shares as of August 31, 2016 and August 31, 2015; Class A ordinary, 33,529,739 and 178,056,462 shares as of August 31, 2016 and August 31, 2015, respectively	(2,591,907)	(11,472,400)
Retained earnings	7,879,980	13,470,008
Accumulated other comprehensive loss	(1,661,720)	(1,411,972)
Total Accenture plc shareholders' equity	7,555,262	6,133,725
Noncontrolling interests	634,114	513,846
Total shareholders' equity	8,189,376	6,647,571
TOTAL LIABILITIES AND SHAREHOLDERS' EQUITY	$ 20,609,004	$ 18,202,647

The accompanying Notes are an integral part of these Consolidated Financial Statements.

Callout notes in figure:
- Arrangement of the years in your template is earliest first. You will need to swap the columns around, when uploading to Excel.
- Your template arranges these sections as follows: Non-Current Assets, Current Assets, and then Current Liabilities. There is also a subtotal for Net current assets/liabilities, as working capital plays a vital part in our model.
- You will need to re-arrange these sections to show Total Non-Current Liabilities and Shareholders Funds

Since we need five years' historical financial statements, we will need to download two more sets of accounts, for the years ended August 31, 2014 (which will include the 2013 figures) and 2012 so that we have accounts for the years 2012 to 2016. This means that you will have to repeat all of the corrections and adjustments on the other two sets of accounts. After correcting for formatting and presentation in the historical accounts, you should convert the historical financials into your template with the earliest year in column **E** followed by the next four years in subsequent columns. You should ensure that the balance check for these historical years is TRUE, which will give you confidence that the historical figures have been completely and accurately imported. The following screenshot illustrates how the balance check shows that the balance sheets are in balance:

	A	B	C	D	E	F	G	H	
1									
2	**Wazobia Global Limited**								
3									
4		Balance Check			*TRUE*	*TRUE*	*TRUE*	*TRUE*	
5									
6		*(Unless otherwise specified, all financials a* Units			Y01A	Y02A	Y03A	Y04F	Y05F
7									
8	ASSUMPTIONS								
9									
10	Revenue Assumptions								
11		Revenue			260,810	272,241	285,009	297,938	
12		Growth %				4%	5%	4.5%	
13		Cost of sales			177,782	184,703	179,052	179,690	
14		Growth %				4%	-3%	0.4%	
15									
16		Sales and marketing expenses			9,204	10,521	11,099	11,210	
17		Sales and mktng exps as a % of Revenue			4%	4%	4%	3.8%	
18		General and administration expenses			25,145	26,402	21,752	26,786	
19		Gen & admin exps as a % of Revenue			10%	10%	8%	9.0%	
20		Other expenses			5,675	13,342	4,394	8,559	
21		Other exps as a % of Revenue			2%	5%	2%	2.9%	
22									
23		Other income			3,333	2,183	2,156	2,156	
24									
25	Balance Sheet Assumptions								
26		Key Ratios							
27		Inventories (Days of cost of sales)				33	41	37	

Projecting the balance sheet and profit and loss account

In order to project the financials, you will need to determine the growth drivers for the balance sheet and profit and loss account. Growth drivers are those parameters that best capture the movement in individual items over the years. The nature of the item and your expertise will determine which parameter you select as an appropriate growth driver. An example of a growth driver for turnover is the year-on-year growth or inflation.

You should know that the balance sheet growth drivers are not as straightforward as with the profit and loss. We will cover this in detail in Chapter 5, *Understanding the Project and Building Assumptions*.

Once the growth drivers have been calculated, you will then need to refer to your notes on the discussions with the management and, in particular, the section heads for their suggestions on how growth is likely to behave in the next five years. An example may be a steady annual increase at the historical **compounded annual growth rate (CAGR)** for the previous five years. The CAGR will be explained in detail in Chapter 5, *Understanding the Project and Building Assumptions*.

Now, we will project the growth drivers for the next five years.

Once you have done that, apply the driver for the first projected year, Y06F, to the actual turnover of the previous year Y05A, which is the final year of historical data, to arrive at the projected turnover for Y06F and so on, as seen in the following screenshot:

Wazobia Global Limited

	Units	Y01A	Y02A	Y03A	Y04A	Y05A	Y06F	Y07F	Y08F	Y08F	Y10F
Balance Check		TRUE	TRUE	TRUE	TRUE	TRUE	FALSE	FALSE	FALSE	FALSE	FALSE
(Unless otherwise specified, all fina											

ASSUMPTIONS

BALANCE SHEET

	Y01A	Y02A	Y03A	Y04A	Y05A	Y06F	Y07F	Y08F	Y08F	Y10F
ASSETS										
Non current assets										
Property, plant and equipment	90,000	80,000	70,000	2,40,000	2,10,000	1,80,000	1,50,000	1,20,000	90,000	60,000
Investments	12,197	11,549	58,106	63,106	58,106	58,106	58,106	58,106	58,106	58,106
Total non current assets	1,02,197	91,549	1,28,106	3,03,106	2,68,106	2,38,106	2,08,106	1,78,106	1,48,106	1,18,106
Current assets										
Inventories	15,545	18,007	21,731	14,530	14,530	20,274	14,778	20,525	15,030	20,779
Trade and other receivables	20,864	31,568	35,901	28,054	28,054	39,026	31,097	42,207	34,423	45,683
Cash and cash equivalents	7,459	17,252	9,265	1,10,863	1,48,306	1,78,435	2,43,864	2,90,573	3,73,372	4,38,279
Total current assets	43,868	66,827	66,897	1,53,447	1,90,890	2,37,736	2,89,739	3,53,305	4,22,825	5,04,741
Current liabilities										
Trade and other payables	12,530	16,054	15,831	14,072	14,072	15,682	14,285	15,896	14,501	16,114
Overdraft	..	..	..	..	..	..	..	..	..	..
Total current liabilites	12,530	16,054	15,831	14,072	14,072	15,682	14,285	15,896	14,501	16,114
Net current assets	31,338	50,773	51,066	1,39,375	1,76,818	2,22,054	2,75,454	3,37,409	4,08,325	4,88,628
Total Assets less current liabilities	1,33,535	1,42,322	1,79,172	4,42,481	4,44,924	4,60,160	4,83,560	5,15,515	5,56,431	6,06,734

Follow this procedure for each of the following years, for each item, to build up the balance sheet and profit and loss account.

Additional schedules and projections

One of the first things you will notice in the preceding screenshot is that the `Balance Check` is now red and `FALSE` for the projected years. This is because our balance sheet and profit and loss account are not yet complete. We have projected growth for most items, but there are certain items that require specific treatment, CapEx, depreciation, loans, and interest.

ASSET SCHEDULE: This schedule is prepared to capture the movement in property, plant, and machinery. The following screenshot shows the full Capex and Depreciation Schedule values:

Wazobia Global Limited

Balance Check		TRUE	TRUE	TRUE	TRUE	TRUE	TRUE	TRUE	TRUE
(Unless otherwise specified, all financials are in N '000, Units		Y01A	Y02A	Y03A	Y04A	Y05A	Y06F	Y07F	Y08F
ASSET SCHEDULE									
Depreciation Method	SLM								
Asset Life	Years	10	10	10	10			10	10
Disposal of Assets	N Mn	-	-	-	-			-	-
Capex	N Mn	100,000	-	-	200,000	-	-	-	-
Depreciation Schedule									
Y01A		10,000	10,000	10,000	10,000	10,000	10,000	10,000	10,000
Y02A									
Y03A									
Y04F					20,000	20,000	20,000	20,000	20,000
Y05F									
Y06F									
Y07F									
Y08F									
Total Depreciation		10,000	10,000	10,000	30,000	30,000	30,000	30,000	30,000
Gross Block									
Opening Balance		-	100,000	100,000	100,000	300,000	300,000	300,000	300,000
Add: Capex		100,000	-	-	200,000	-	-	-	-
Less: Assets Sold/ Disposed		-	-	-	-	-	-	-	-
Closing Balance		100,000	100,000	100,000	300,000	300,000	300,000	300,000	300,000
Accumulated Depreciation									
Opening Balance		-	10,000	20,000	30,000	60,000	90,000	120,000	150,000
Add: Depreciation during current year		10,000	10,000	10,000	30,000	30,000	30,000	30,000	30,000
Closing Balance		10,000	20,000	30,000	60,000	90,000	120,000	150,000	180,000
Net Book Value		90,000	80,000	70,000	240,000	210,000	180,000	150,000	120,000

The company's plans for CapEx over the duration of the model will be reflected here. Historical CapEx and disposal of assets will be shown under the years during which the expenditure or sale took place. The schedule will also take into account the cost of the assets and useful life and depreciation rates and methods. Assets with different depreciation rates will be treated separately.

The ultimate destination of this schedule is the end of year total cost of fixed assets, accumulated depreciation charge. These will be arrived at using the BASE method. These balances are taken to the balance sheet. Another important output of this schedule is the total depreciation for the year that is taken to the profit and loss account.

DEBT SCHEDULE: The debt schedule is prepared to map the movement in secured and unsecured loans. Here, again, using the BASE method, we arrive at the closing balances that are taken to the balance sheet. The schedule is also used to calculate the interest charge for the year, which is taken to the profit and loss account. The following screenshot is an illustration of the debt schedule and other schedules used to update the balance sheet and profit and loss account:

Wazobia Global Limited

Balance Check		TRUE	TRUE	TRUE	TRUE	TRUE	TRUE	TRUE	TRUE
(Unless otherwise specified	Units	Y01A	Y02A	Y03A	Y04A	Y05A	Y06F	Y07F	Y08F
DEBT SCHEDULE									
Unsecured Loans									
Opening		-	40,000	35,000	30,000	2,75,000	2,70,000	2,65,000	2,60,000
Additions		40,000	-	-	2,50,000	-	-	-	-
Repayments 0n 40M	8 yrs		5,000	5,000	5,000	5,000	5,000	5,000	5,000
Repayments 0n 250M	10 yrs								
Closing	0	40,000	35,000	30,000	2,75,000	2,70,000	2,65,000	2,60,000	2,55,000
Interest rate		10%	10%	10%	10%	10%	10%	10%	10%
Interest		2,000	3,750	3,250	15,250	27,250	26,750	26,250	25,750
SOCI - OTHER CALCN									
Equity									
Opening		70,000	70,000	70,000	70,000	70,000	70,000	70,000	70,000
Additions		-	-	-	-	-	-	-	-
Closing		70,000	70,000	70,000	70,000	70,000	70,000	70,000	70,000
Retained earnings									
Opening		-	18,535	32,322	74,172	87,481	99,924	1,20,160	1,48,560
Result for the year - PAT		18,535	13,787	41,850	13,309	12,443	20,236	28,401	36,955
Closing		18,535	32,322	74,172	87,481	99,924	1,20,160	1,48,560	1,85,515
RATIOS									

Changes in equity: Equity is represented by share capital and accumulated reserves that have not been distributed. Additions to share capital will be reflected here, as well as movement in reserves as a result of profit or loss for the year and dividends and other distributions. The final balances of share capital and reserves are taken to the balance sheet.

Cash flow statement

At this stage, our profit and loss accounts for the projected years are now completely populated. However, our balance check is still showing a red FALSE, indicating that there is something missing from the balance sheet. Unlike other items, it is not possible to project cash. The cash balance is a fallout from all transactions carried out during the period under review. This fact is captured in the cash flow statement, which considers the inflows and outflows of cash. The net result is then applied to the opening cash balance to arrive at the closing cash balance at the period end. The following screenshot shows a completed cash flow statement, which ends with a closing balance for cash, which is taken to the balance sheet:

Wazobia Global Limited

Balance Check			TRUE	TRUE	TRUE	TRUE	TRUE	TRUE	TRUE	TRUE
(Unless otherwise specified,	Units		YO1A	YO2A	YO3A	YO4A	YO5A	YO6F	YO7F	YO8F
CASH FLOW STATEMENT										
Cashflow from Operating Activities										
PAT			13,787	41,850	13,309	12,443	20,236	28,401	36,955
Add: Depreciation			10,000	10,000	30,000	30,000	30,000	30,000	30,000
Add: Interest Expense			3,750	3,250	15,250	27,250	26,750	26,250	25,750
Net Change in Working Capital										
Add: Increase in Accounts payable			3,524	(223)	(1,759)	-	1,610	(1,397)	1,611
Less: Increase in Inventory			(2,462)	(3,724)	7,201	0	(5,745)	5,496	(5,747)
Less: Increase in Account Receivables			(10,704)	(4,333)	7,847	-	(10,972)	7,929	(11,110)
Net Change in Working Capital			(9,642)	(8,280)	13,290	0	(15,107)	12,028	(15,245)
Cashflow from Operations			17,895	46,820	71,849	69,693	61,879	96,678	77,460
Cashflow from Investment Activities										
Less: Capex			-	-	(2,00,000)	-	-	-	-
Add: Proceeds from Disposal of Assets						-	-	-	
Less: Increase in WIP						-	-	-	
Less: Increase in Investments			648	(46,557)	(5,000)	5,000	-	-	-
Cashflow from Investment Activities			648	(46,557)	(2,05,000)	5,000	-	-	-
Cashflow from Financing Activities										
Add: New Equity Raised										
Add: New Unsecured Loans Raised			-	-	2,50,000			-	-
Less: Unsecured Loans Repaid			(5,000)	(5,000)	(5,000)	(5,000)	(5,000)	(5,000)	(5,000)
Less: Dividends Paid										
Less: Interest Expense			(3,750)	(3,250)	(15,250)	(27,250)	(26,750)	(26,250)	(25,750)
Cashflow from Financing Activities			(8,750)	(8,250)	2,29,750	(32,250)	(31,750)	(31,250)	(30,750)
Net Cashflow			9,793	(7,987)	96,599	42,443	30,129	65,428	46,710
Cash Balance										
Opening Balance			7,459	17,252	9,265	1,05,864	1,48,306	1,78,435	2,43,864
Net Cashflow			9,793	(7,987)	96,599	42,443	30,129	65,428	46,710
Closing Balance			17,252	9,265	1,05,864	1,48,306	1,78,435	2,43,864	2,90,573

When the closing cash balance is taken to the balance sheet, the balance check for the projected years should now show a white TRUE on a green background, giving some assurance that calculations up till that point are correct. The cash flow statement is one of the most important statements for a company. To most investment analysts, cash is king. You may wonder why you need another statement that looks similar to a rearranged balance sheet. Remember that the accounts are prepared on the accrual basis of accounting.

This means that part of the turnover shown in the profit and loss account may not yet have been converted into cash. For example, at the year end, some customers may not yet have paid for goods purchased from you on credit. Similarly, expenses are recorded when incurred even though you may not yet have paid for them, for example, expenses usually paid in arrears such as electricity or goods you have purchased on credit.

The cash flow statement is constructed to extract cash inflows and outflows from the balance sheet and profit and loss account. The statement shows, separately, cash flow from operations, cash flow from investing activities, and cash flow from financing activities. You would expect cash generated from operations to be regularly greater than net income. If the reverse is the case, you would want to know why there is a delay in converting income into cash. The section on investing activities shows the movement in long term assets, such as long-term investments and property, plant, and equipment.

Fresh loans and repayment of existing loans, as well as movement in share capital will be reflected under financing activities. In order to maintain a healthy dividend policy, repay loans, and have funds for expansion, a company needs to consistently generate more cash than it utilizes.

Preparing ratio analysis

With the preparation of a cash flow statement, we now have the core content of a set of financial statements. These financial statements, now referred to as a statement of financial position, statement of comprehensive income, and cash flow statement, along with explanatory notes and schedules, are distributed to shareholders of the company and government. It is also these financial statements that are available to other interest groups such as investors and holders of the debt capital of the company.

The financial statements provide a significant amount of information about the company and its results for the period under review. However, on their own, they are not adequate for decision making. Ratio analysis provides an in-depth look at the details behind the figures. The following screenshot is an example of a set of ratio analysis:

Wazobia Global Limited									
Balance Check		*TRUE*	*TRUE*	*TRUE*	*TRUE*	*TRUE*	*TRUE*	*TRUE*	*TRUE*
(Unless otherwise specified, all financials are in N '000, Units		Y01A	Y02A	Y03A	Y04A	Y05A	Y06F	Y07F	Y08F
ASSET SCHEDULE									
Depreciation Method	SLM								
Asset Life	Years	10	10	10	10			10	10
Disposal of Assets	N Mn	-	-	-	-			-	-
Capex	N Mn	100,000	-	-	200,000	-	-	-	-
Depreciation Schedule									
Y01A		10,000	10,000	10,000	10,000	10,000	10,000	10,000	10,000
Y02A									
Y03A									
Y04F					20,000	20,000	20,000	20,000	20,000
Y05F									
Y06F									
Y07F									
Y08F									
Total Depreciation		10,000	10,000	10,000	30,000	30,000	30,000	30,000	30,000
Gross Block									
Opening Balance		-	100,000	100,000	100,000	300,000	300,000	300,000	300,000
Add: Capex		100,000	-	-	200,000	-	-	-	-
Less: Assets Sold/ Disposed		-	-	-	-	-	-	-	-
Closing Balance		100,000	100,000	100,000	300,000	300,000	300,000	300,000	300,000
Accumulated Depreciation									
Opening Balance		-	10,000	20,000	30,000	60,000	90,000	120,000	150,000
Add: Depreciation during current year		10,000	10,000	10,000	30,000	30,000	30,000	30,000	30,000
Closing Balance		10,000	20,000	30,000	60,000	90,000	120,000	150,000	180,000
Net Book Value		90,000	80,000	70,000	240,000	210,000	180,000	150,000	120,000

By looking at the relationship between strategic pairs of figures from the accounts, ratio analysis can provide insights about the profitability, liquidity, efficiency, and debt management of a company for the year, as well as over a period of time. The ratios in the preceding screenshot are by no means exhaustive. There is a vast array of ratios to choose from and different modelers will have their own preferences.

However, what is important is that you should be able to interpret whichever ratios you choose to include in such a way as to provide qualitative assistance to the decision-making process.

Valuation

There are two main approaches to valuation, which are as follows:

- **Relative approach**: In this approach, you have the following methods:
    - **The comparative company method of valuation**: This method obtains the value of a business by looking at the value of similar businesses and their trading multiples, the most common of which is **enterprise value (EV)** and **earnings before interest, tax, depreciation, and amortization (EBITDA)**, where EV is divided by EBITDA.
    - **The precedent transaction method**: Here, you compare the business to other similar businesses in the industry that have recently been sold or acquired. Again, you can use multiples to derive a value for your business or company.

- **Absolute approach**: This approach estimates all future free cash flow of the company and discounts it back to today. It is called the **discounted cash flow (DCF)** method. Essentially, the approach considers that the worth of a company can be equated to the amount of cash it can generate after considering the following:

    - Free cash flow
    - Time value of money
    - Discount factor
    - Cost of capital
    - Weighted average cost of capital
    - Terminal growth rate
    - Terminal value

These technical concepts will be explained in greater detail in Chapter 9, *Valuation*. The DCF method usually results in the highest value for the entity but is widely considered to be the most accurate. In order to give meaning to the different results obtained for the value of the company, you would then plot them all to obtain a range of values that can be interpreted in a number of ways.

Typically, the company will be said to be undervalued if it is quoted at a price lower than the lowest value calculated and overvalued if it is quoted at a price higher than the highest value calculated. Where a single value is required, the mean of all of the calculated values can be taken.

Summary

In this chapter, we looked at the steps to be followed in building a financial model. We understood why it is necessary to have a systematic approach. We went through the steps from discussions with management through to calculating a valuation of the enterprise and the shares of the company, understanding the purpose and importance of each step.

In the next chapter, we will look at how we can use Excel formulas and functions to speed up our work and make modeling a more rewarding experience.

Section 2: The Use of Excel - Features and Functions for Financial Modeling

In this section, you will learn about the various tools and features of Excel that are regularly used in financial modeling. These will be explained in detail to allow you to start using them confidently.

This section comprises the following chapters:

- Chapter 3, *Formulas and Functions – Completing Modeling Tasks with a Single Formula*
- Chapter 4, *Applying the Referencing Framework in Excel*

3

Formulas and Functions - Completing Modeling Tasks with a Single Formula

One of the first things that makes Excel more than a glorified electronic calculator is its use of functions and formulas. This feature allows Excel to combine a number of mathematical tasks—some of which can be quite complex—into a single function. In this chapter, you will learn how to use formulas and will understand a selection of the most widely used functions.

The following topics will be covered in this chapter:

- Understanding functions and formulas
- Working with lookup functions
- Utility functions
- Pivot tables and charts
- Pitfalls to avoid

Understanding functions and formulas

In order to enter either a formula or a function, you must first type =. A **formula** is a statement that includes one or more operands (+, -, /, *, and ^), such as =34+7 or =A3-G5 (this formula subtracts the contents of cell G5 from the contents of cell A3). A function can also be included as part of a formula, such as =SUM(B3:B7)*A3.

A **function** is a command that contains a series of instructions for Excel to carry out. A function contains one or more arguments, inviting the user to specify the input cell or range of cells on which the instructions are to be carried out, for example, MATCH(A5, F4:F23,false).

A function can include a formula as part of an argument, such as =IF(A4*B4>C4,D4,E4).

However, the distinction between them is often ignored and the term formula is used to indicate either a formula or function.

To enter a formula, we start with the = sign followed by the name of a function and then open brackets. While in edit mode, an on-screen guide is displayed just below the text, showing the arguments to be specified. Each argument is separated from the next with a comma and the first argument appears in bold font as it is the active argument. Once you have specified the input for an argument, press the comma (,) key. The bold highlight moves onto the next argument as that is now the active argument. When all inputs have been specified, we close the brackets to end the formula.

Working with lookup functions

Lookup functions are some of the most widely used functions in Excel. Generally, the intention is to fetch a value from one table (the source) to the active cell in which you are typing the formula (the target). Essentially, the function guides Excel to identify a row and column in the source table. The intersection of that row and column will give you the source cell whose value you want to extract. For example, say you have a sales report that includes data for various products sold within a specified period and you wish to populate a field, Product Cost, with the cost of each of the products in your report.

The following screenshot is a sample sales report showing details of daily sales including Product, Salesperson, and other details:

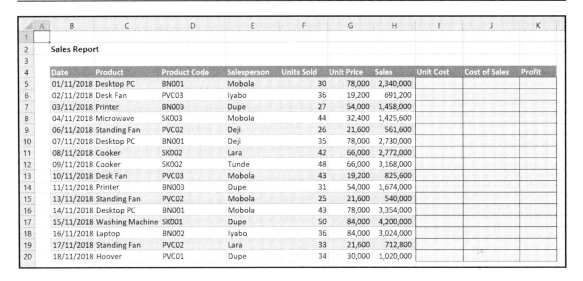

Unit Cost for each product can be obtained from a products database.

You could use a lookup function to locate the individual products in the products database and then retrieve the associated cost. We will also refer to this table, Products Database, as our source table. The following screenshot is a sample Products Database table showing the product codes and unit costs of each product:

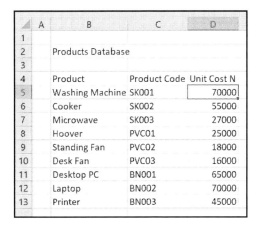

In order to ensure that your lookup selects the correct item, you must use a unique lookup value that appears in both tables, a value that will uniquely identify each record. People could have the same name, so you would use employee IDs rather than employee names; similarly, product names could be duplicated, so you would use Product Code instead.

There are a number of lookup functions, each of them having particular scenarios to which they are best suited. We will have a look at some of the more popular ones.

The VLOOKUP function

The arguments for VLOOKUP are shown in the following screenshot:

Unit Cost	Cost of Sales	Profit		
=VLOOKUP(D5,'Prod Dbase'!C4:D13,2,FALSE				
	VLOOKUP(lookup_value, table_array, col_index_num, **[range_lookup]**)			

Any argument enclosed in square brackets, [], is optional; therefore, if no value is entered for that argument, a default value is taken. Values must be entered for all other arguments; otherwise, the formula will result in an error.

For the VLOOKUP function, the optional argument is range_lookup. This requires you to select True if you are looking for an approximate match for your lookup value or False if you are looking for an exact match. Excel allows you to substitute 1 for True and 0 for False. If no value is selected, then the argument defaults to False.

This function tells Excel to find the lookup value in the first column from the left of the lookup array that you specify. Note that this may not be the first column of the source table.

In our example, the lookup value is a product code; therefore, for the first record in our sales report, the lookup value is BN001, which is in cell **D5**. The following screenshot shows the construction of the VLOOKUP formula in the Sales Report table:

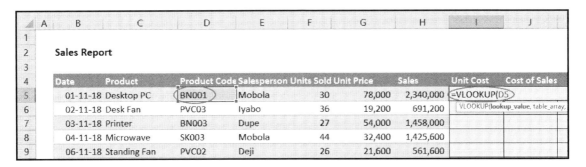

Our lookup array must start from column **C** in the Products Database table as this is where the Product Code field lies—note that this is the second column of the Products Database table. Excel will then locate the position of the lookup value in this first column, as shown in the following screenshot:

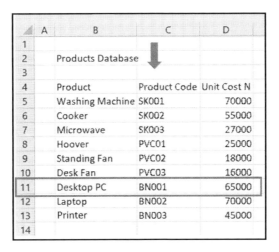

From the preceding screenshot, we can see that product BN001 is in row **11** of the Products Database table, in the Product Code field.

The next argument is the `column_index_num` (column index number) value, which refers to the position of the source field in the lookup array, starting from the unique field as column **1**. The **source field** is the field from which you want to retrieve data. In our example, the source field is `Unit Cost`, which is column **D**, the second column of our lookup array. This gives us `col_index_num` of 2:

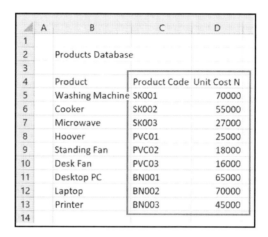

In this way, we have identified column **D** and row **11** for the source cell. Excel will then retrieve the data from cell **D11** (65,000) and place it in our target cell in the `Sales Report` table:

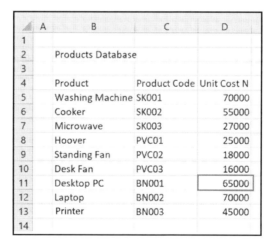

Once you have completed your formula and successfully extracted the unit cost for the first record in our Sales Report table, copy the formula down the column for the other records in the Sales Report table.

The INDEX function

The INDEX and MATCH functions are usually used together. The INDEX function has the arguments to specify the row and column of the source cell. In order to make the formula dynamic, you substitute MATCH for the INDEX argument, for the row, column, or both. This is a very powerful formula that has arguments for both arrays and simple formulas:

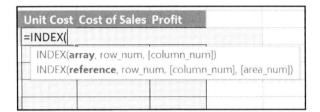

The first line of arguments of the INDEX formula is for the array range. Array formulas return a range of values as opposed to just one—as is the case with simple formulas. We will touch on array formulas later in this book, but for now, we will concentrate on simple formulas.

The second line of arguments is for the reference form. The first argument requires the reference that is similar to the lookup array in VLOOKUP. In simple index formulas, this could be restricted to a range of cells within one column (or within one row).

If you restrict the index reference to one column, you have effectively identified the column of the source cell. In our example, we have selected cells D5 to D13 as our reference:

	× ✓ *fx*	=INDEX('Prod Dbase'!$D$5:$D$13				
A	B	C	D	E	F	G	H
			INDEX(**array**, row_num, [column_num])			
	Products Database		INDEX(**reference**, row_num, [column_num], [area_num])			
	Product	Product Code	Unit Cost N			
	Washing Machine	SK001	70000			
	Cooker	SK002	55000			
	Microwave	SK003	27000			
	Hoover	PVC01	25000			
	Standing Fan	PVC02	18000			
	Desk Fan	PVC03	16000			
	Desktop PC	BN001	65000			
	Laptop	BN002	70000			
	Printer	BN003	45000			

The next argument is row_num. In order to substitute it for the row argument, you will need to embed the MATCH function within the INDEX function, which is still active. To do this, just start typing the new function after the comma. As long as you have not yet entered the final parentheses for a function, Excel recognizes that the formula is still active, so there is no need to type = again.

The MATCH function

The first argument in the MATCH function is the lookup_value argument, which you look for in the lookup array. In this case, however, there is no restriction as to the location of the lookup array. We are using the same lookup value as in the VLOOKUP example, BN001, in cell **D5** of the Sales Report worksheet.

Here, again, as shown in the following screenshot, you can restrict the lookup array to one column. In our example, we know that the match for our lookup values are under the Product Code field in column **C** of the Products Database worksheet. We therefore select cells C5 to C13 as our lookup array:

◢	A	B	C	D	E
1		MATCH(lookup_value, **lookup_array**, [match_type])			
2		Products Database			
3					
4		Product	Product Code	Unit Cost N	
5		Washing Machine	SK001	70000	
6		Cooker	SK002	55000	
7		Microwave	SK003	27000	
8		Hoover	PVC01	25000	
9		Standing Fan	PVC02	18000	
10		Desk Fan	PVC03	16000	
11		Desktop PC	BN001	65000	
12		Laptop	BN002	70000	
13		Printer	BN003	45000	
14				9R x 1C	

Note that the MATCH lookup array must start from the same worksheet row as the reference in the INDEX function. In our example, they both start from worksheet row **5**. You end the match formula with match_type, which is the same as range_lookup in the VLOOKUP function. You need to specify whether you want an approximate match, less than (1), greater than the lookup value (-1), or an exact match (0).

The MATCH function returns an integer that corresponds to the position of the row within the lookup array in which the lookup value is found. This should not be mistaken for the worksheet row number.

In our example, the MATCH function will return the number 7 because the lookup value, BN001, is found in the 7th row of our lookup array—worksheet row **11**. As soon as you close the final bracket of the MATCH formula, Excel takes you back to the INDEX function.

The next argument is column_num. As we have already determined the column number by restricting our reference to one column, we can ignore this argument. The final argument, area_num, is for more complex situations where we introduce a third dimension after row and column, such as multiple tables with the same field layouts. Again, we can ignore this argument as we will not be using it.

Having identified row **7** and column **D**, we now have the source cell, **D11**, which returns the value of 65000. You will note that INDEX and MATCH overcome the restriction in VLOOKUP, where the unique field must be the first column of the lookup array.

As a result, many users prefer to use INDEX and MATCH, even where VLOOKUP would work. Those who are intimidated by the function combination of INDEX and MATCH prefer to stick to VLOOKUP and would rather change the order of table columns to make it suitable for VLOOKUP.

The CHOOSE function

The CHOOSE function allows you to create a list of values or actions to perform and then select which value to use or action to perform, by choosing a number corresponding to the position of the values or actions in the list. The syntax for CHOOSE—as shown in the following screenshot—has two arguments: index_num, then the list of values or actions shown as value1, value2, and so on.

This screenshot shows the arguments of the CHOOSE function:

In the example shown here, we want to show the results separately from the average and median of the product unit costs in the Products Database worksheet. We first set up data validation in an empty cell, so that the values of 1 or 2 can be selected by clicking the drop-down arrow that appears beside the cell. The cell with the data validation will be index_num of the CHOOSE formula. This is a screenshot of the data validation:

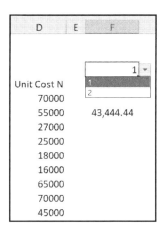

We then list the actions to choose from. In this case, we have the average or the median. If we list them in that order, then if index_num shows 1, the average will be selected, and if it shows 2, then median will be selected. The following screenshot shows the complete CHOOSE formula:

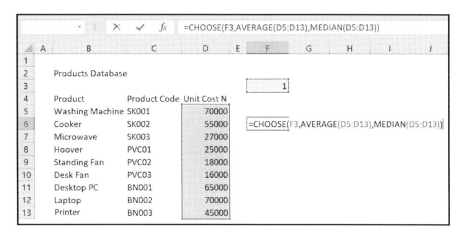

When the index number is 1, the AVERAGE function is selected, and it returns the value 43,444.44. This is a screenshot of the CHOOSE function with Index_Num as 1:

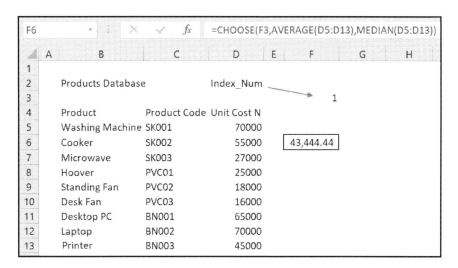

When the index number is 2, the MEDIAN function is selected, and it returns the value 45,000.00. This is a screenshot of the CHOOSE function with Index_Num as 2:

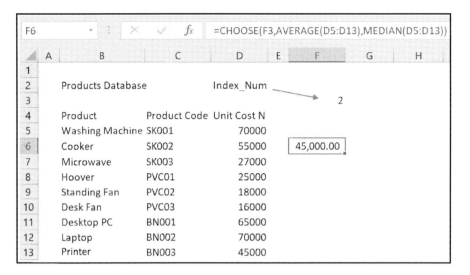

Implementing the CHOOSE function

Let's assume that you are tracking the financial records of your company and your boss wants you to deliver two reports every week, containing the total amount of sales that you made for a particular week and the total amount of purchases you made toward the company's stores. How would you go about it?

You can always select all of the instances of sales and then calculate the sum of them. Once that is done, you have to again select all instances of purchases made and find the sum of purchases too. Having to do so frequently would be really time-consuming and boring. Here's where the CHOOSE function comes into play! We can implement a simple model that does everything for you in one click, using the following steps:

1. Load all of the required values that you need to account for and compile them into a table, as seen here:

Product	Sale	Purchase
Washing Machine	75000	70000
Cooker	5420	55000
Microwave	78924	27000
Hoover	1111	25000
Standing Fan	10000	18000
Desk Fan	15000	16000
Desktop PC	19000	65000
Laptop	100000	70000
Printer	11000	45000

2. We will now start writing the CHOOSE function:

Products Database				Index_Num	
				2	
Product	Sales	Purchases			
Washing Machine	75000	70000			
Cooker	5420	55000		=CHOOSE()	
Microwave	78924	27000		CHOOSE(index_num, value1, [value2], ...)	
Hoover	1111	25000			
Standing Fan	10000	18000			
Desk Fan	15000	16000			
Desktop PC	19000	65000			
Laptop	100000	70000			
Printer	11000	45000			

3. The first value we need to enter is the cell where we have put the options, which, in our case, is F4:

Products Database			Index_Num	
			2	
Product	**Sales**	**Purchases**		
Washing Machine	75000	70000		
Cooker	5420	55000	=CHOOSE(F4)	
Microwave	78924	27000	CHOOSE(index_num, value1, [value2], ...)	
Hoover	1111	25000		
Standing Fan	10000	18000		
Desk Fan	15000	16000		
Desktop PC	19000	65000		
Laptop	100000	70000		
Printer	11000	45000		

4. Now, we will assign two options to F4, 1 and 2, using data validation. We will now edit the formula so that if we select 1, the cell where the formula is input will display the sum of all of the sales made for that week, and if we select 2, it will display the sum of all of the purchases. So, first we will select all of the cells in the Sales column, C6 to C14, and input it into the formula cell as SUM(C6:C14), as seen here:

Products Database			Index_Num	
			2	
Product	**Sales**	**Purchases**		
Washing Machine	75000	70000		
Cooker	5420	55000	=CHOOSE(F4,SUM(C6:C14))	
Microwave	78924	27000	SUM(number1, [number2], ...)	
Hoover	1111	25000		
Standing Fan	10000	18000		
Desk Fan	15000	16000		
Desktop PC	19000	65000		
Laptop	100000	70000		
Printer	11000	45000		

5. Next, we will select all of the cells in the `Purchases` column and input those into the next field of the formula as `SUM(D6:D14)`, as follows:

Products Database			Index_Num	
			2	
Product	**Sales**	**Purchases**		
Washing Machine	75000	70000		
Cooker	5420	55000	=CHOOSE(F4,SUM(C6:C14),SUM(D6:D14))	
Microwave	78924	27000	SUM(number1, [number2], ...)	
Hoover	1111	25000		
Standing Fan	10000	18000		
Desk Fan	15000	16000		
Desktop PC	19000	65000		
Laptop	100000	70000		
Printer	11000	45000		

6. This results in the following output:

Products Database			Index_Num	
			1	
Product	**Sales**	**Purchases**		
Washing Machine	75000	70000		
Cooker	5420	55000	Total Cost	
Microwave	78924	27000	315,455.00	
Hoover	1111	25000		
Standing Fan	10000	18000		
Desk Fan	15000	16000		
Desktop PC	19000	65000		
Laptop	100000	70000		
Printer	11000	45000		

Now, as seen in the preceding screenshot, when 1 is selected, the cost of sales becomes visible, which, in our case, is 315,455.00.

7. If we select 2, we will get the cost of purchases, as seen here:

Products Database			Index_Num
			2
Product	**Sales**	**Purchases**	
Washing Machine	75000	70000	
Cooker	5420	55000	Total Cost
Microwave	78924	27000	391,000.00
Hoover	1111	25000	
Standing Fan	10000	18000	
Desk Fan	15000	16000	
Desktop PC	19000	65000	
Laptop	100000	70000	
Printer	11000	45000	

This is just a basic scenario in which the function can come in handy. This will be particularly useful when you have large amounts of data that needs to be filtered and sorted.

Utility functions

Utility functions can be used on their own. However, they come into their own when embedded in other, more complex functions. In such cases, they expand the scope and functionality of the enclosing function by providing access to more conditions or variables.

Some examples of utility functions are IF, AND, OR, MAX, MIN, and MATCH. We will now look at a few of them here.

The IF function

This is one of the most widely used functions in Excel. It can be used on its own or as part of another formula. The IF function checks whether a condition is met, then returns one value if it is and another value if it isn't. The syntax contains three arguments:

- logical_test: The logical test is a statement that returns a value of true if the condition is met, or false if the condition is not met.

- `value_if_true`: This argument allows you to specify which value you wish to be returned if the condition is met and the result of the logical test is `true`.
- `value_if_false`: This argument allows you to specify which value you wish to be returned if the condition is not met and the result of the logical test is `false`.

Say you want to reward your salespersons with 2% of sales whenever the profit exceeds 300,000. You could write an `IF` formula to automate this. The logical test would be the statement—profit is greater than 300,000. In the following example, for the first record, this is K5>K2. The statement will either be `true` or `false`. If the result is `true`, the value to return is then `Sales` × `Commission` (2%). In our example, this is H5*H2. If the result is `false`, then the value returned will be 0. The following screenshot is an illustration of the `IF` formula:

F	G	H	I	J	K	L	M	N	O	P
	Bonus on Sales	2%		**Hurdle**	300,000					
Sold	**Unit Price**	**Sales**	**Unit Cost**	**Cost of Sales**	**Profit**		**IF**	**MAX**	**MIN**	
30	78,000	2,340,000	65,000	1,950,000	390,000		=IF(K5>$K$2,$H$5*H2,0			
36	19,200	691,200	16,000	576,000	115,200		IF(logical_test, [value_if_true], **[value_if_false]**)			
27	54,000	1,458,000	45,000	1,215,000	243,000					
44	32,400	1,425,600	27,000	1,188,000	237,600					
26	21,600	561,600	18,000	468,000	93,600					

The MAX and MIN functions

These functions are used to select either the maximum (`MAX`) or minimum (`MIN`) from a list of values. With a bit of imagination, you can put the `MAX` or `MIN` formulas to very efficient use.

For example, in your financial model, `Cash Balance` can turn out to be positive or negative. A positive balance would be posted to the `Cash In Hand` account on the asset side of the balance sheet, while a negative balance would be shown as `Overdraft` under current liabilities. If we simply related `Cash In Hand` or `Overdraft` to `Cash Balance`, then we could either have a negative balance displayed as `Cash In Hand` or a positive balance displayed as `Overdraft`.

A way around this is to use the MAX and MIN formulas as shown in the following screenshot:

▲	A	B	C	D	E	F
1						
2						
3		**Cash Balance**	**Cash In Hand**	**Overdraft**		
4		1,450,422	=MAX(B4,0			
5		663,315	MAX(number1, **[number2]**, [number3], ...)			
6		(349,661)				
7		779,461				

In the preceding screenshot, we are asking the MAX formula to display the greater value of Cash Balance and 0. A positive cash balance will always be greater than 0 and will hence be displayed as Cash In Hand. However, whenever the cash balance is negative, since this will always be less than 0, Cash In Hand will display 0.

The following screenshot is an illustration of the MIN function:

▲	A	B	C	D	E	F	G
1							
2							
3		**Cash Balance**	**Cash In Hand**	**Overdraft**			
4		1,450,422	1,450,422	=MIN(B4,0			
5		663,315	663,315	MIN(number1, **[number2]**, [number3], ...)			
6		(349,661)	-				
7		779,461	779,461				
8		(393,443)	-				
9		717,832	717,832				
10		15,107	15,107				
11		(418,702)	-				

In this case, we use the MIN formula to ensure that only negative cash balances will be displayed as Overdraft, since a negative cash balance will always be less than 0.

By copying the formulas, we can see how the cash balances have been neatly and accurately classified as Cash In Hand and Overdraft, as shown in the following screenshot, which shows the full result after applying the MAX and MIN formulas:

	A	B	C	D
1				
2				
3		Cash Balance	Cash In Hand	Overdraft
4		1,450,422	1,450,422	-
5		663,315	663,315	-
6		(349,661)	-	(349,661)
7		779,461	779,461	-
8		(393,443)	-	(393,443)
9		717,832	717,832	-
10		15,107	15,107	-
11		(418,702)	-	(418,702)
12		49,887	49,887	-
13		86,528	86,528	-
14		868,678	868,678	-
15		(319,840)	-	(319,840)
16		8,606	8,606	-
17		754,551	754,551	-
18		784,338	784,338	-
19		681,504	681,504	-
20				

Implementing the functions

We will now implement the MAX and MIN functions to the Marks.xlsx file used in Chapter
4, *Applying the Referencing Framework in Excel*. We will use the MAX function to find the
highest score in the class and the MIN function to find the lowest using the following steps:

1. First, we will create two independent cells that we will use to display the highest
   and lowest scores, as follows:

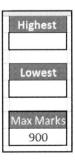

2. Now, to find the student with the highest score, we will find the biggest value in the `Percentage` column, by using the following formula:

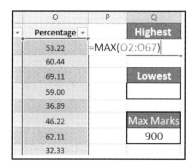

This results in the following output:

3. Similarly, we need to find the minimum marks scored by a student by using the following formula:

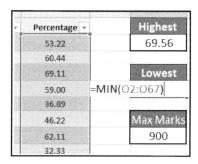

This results in the following output:

This shows how useful these functions can be, especially when you have a huge number of entries to sort through.

Pivot tables and charts

Pivot tables are one of the most powerful tools in Excel. A pivot table can summarize little or large amounts of data into a compact form, which reveals trends and relationships that were not apparent from looking at the original data.

The pivot table allows you to introduce conditions based on the original data so that you can view the summarized data from different perspectives. It does all of this without you having to type any formulas. Most users are under the impression that pivot table reports are complex and difficult to prepare; but in reality, the complexity is behind the scenes and taken care of by Excel. All you have to do is follow a few simple guidelines and you will be able to produce complex pivot tables with ease.

The first step is to ensure that your data is in the proper Excel table format, bearing in mind that you may have to work with data prepared by someone else.

Excel identification and navigation shortcuts depend on your table being in the proper format. Most actions require the specification of the target range. Excel can correctly identify the required range and isolate the field headers, but only if the data is in the proper table format, which can be seen in the following screenshot:

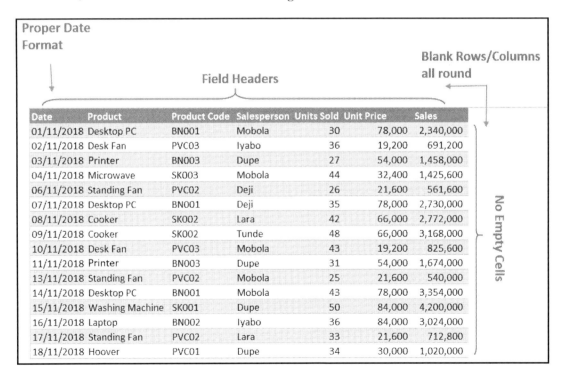

In database terminology, each column of the table represents a field, and each row (apart from the first row) represents a record. The first row of the table should contain the field headers. There should be no empty cells in the table and no duplicate records.

Excel is very efficient at detecting data types and handling different forms of date format, including 15/01/2019, 15-Jan-19, 15-01-2019, 01-15-2019, and 2019-01-15, among others. However, Excel is very sensitive and any slight anomaly in the data may produce erratic results. For example, if you inadvertently type a leading space before the date—as in the image on the left-hand side of the following screenshot—Excel treats it as a General data type.

The image on the right-hand side of the following screenshot shows the same text without the leading space; therefore, Excel correctly recognizes it as a date and automatically assigns the Date format to the cell:

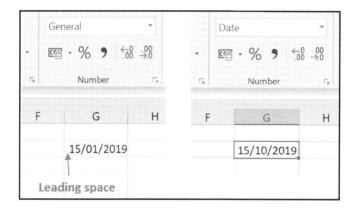

The reason for explaining this in detail is because pivot tables have a special relationship with date and other data types. If a date field is included in your table, the pivot table will recognize it and allow you to group the dates into days, months, quarters, and years. However, if just one cell of the date field has an anomaly—like in the preceding example—the pivot table will not recognize it as a date and the group option will be unavailable. Once your data has been cleaned up and prepared, you are ready to create a pivot table. Ensure that the cursor is in any cell within the table, then press *Insert* and select **PivotTable** from the **Tables** group. The **Create PivotTable** dialog box is launched. You will be required to select a range and then a location for the pivot table report. Excel will usually intelligently guess the correct range for the pivot table; but if it doesn't, you can manually select the required range.

Although you can place the pivot table on the same sheet as the source data, this can sometimes become congested. By default, Excel will create the pivot table on a new worksheet. Again, you can override this, if you wish, and specify a location on either the same or another worksheet:

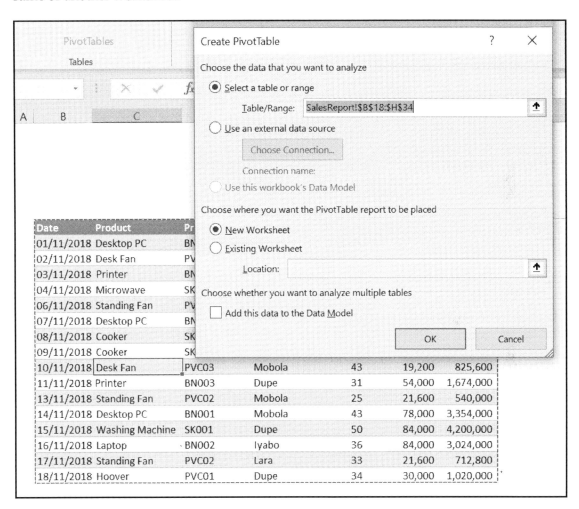

When you press **OK**, a pivot table will be created. Initially, only the field list will be populated with the names of all of the fields in your table, which will be arranged vertically with checkboxes beside them. Below that, there are four boxes, titled **Filters**, **Columns**, **Rows**, and **Values**. You build the table by dragging the field names to the boxes as desired.

Before you start building your table, it would help if you try and envisage the layout you desire. The **Values** box is best suited for numerical fields, so you would drag the `Sales` field to this box, resulting in the updated table shown in the following screenshot, which shows how the **Values** field is displayed in the pivot table:

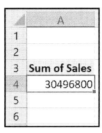

As you have not yet specified a condition or criteria, Excel simply totals the **Values** field and calls it `Sum of Sales`. You may then wish to display the sales per salesperson for each product. The following screenshot shows sales per salesperson:

Row Labels	Sum of Sales
⊟ Cooker	5940000
Lara	2772000
Tunde	3168000
⊟ Desk Fan	1516800
Iyabo	691200
Mobola	825600
⊟ Desktop PC	8424000
Deji	2730000
Mobola	5694000
⊟ Hoover	1020000
Dupe	1020000
⊟ Laptop	3024000
Iyabo	3024000
⊟ Microwave	1425600
Mobola	1425600
⊟ Printer	3132000
Dupe	3132000
⊟ Standing Fan	1814400
Deji	561600
Lara	712800
Mobola	540000
⊟ Washing Machine	4200000
Dupe	4200000
Grand Total	30496800

For the previous screenshot, the field list would look like this:

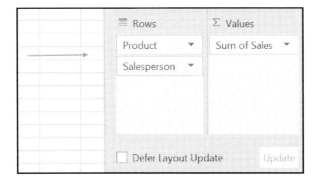

Alternatively, you may wish to show the sales of products per salesperson, as shown in the following screenshot:

Row Labels	Sum of Sales
Deji	**3291600**
Desktop PC	2730000
Standing Fan	561600
Dupe	**8352000**
Hoover	1020000
Printer	3132000
Washing Machine	4200000
Iyabo	**3715200**
Desk Fan	691200
Laptop	3024000
Lara	**3484800**
Cooker	2772000
Standing Fan	712800
Mobola	**8485200**
Desk Fan	825600
Desktop PC	5694000
Microwave	1425600
Standing Fan	540000
Tunde	**3168000**
Cooker	3168000
Grand Total	**30496800**

Notice that the positions of the `Product` and `Salesperson` fields are reversed in the rows box, as shown in the following screenshot:

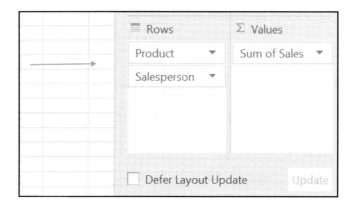

An alternative layout could be achieved by displaying the products horizontally. This can be done by dragging the product field to the **Columns** box instead of the **Rows** box:

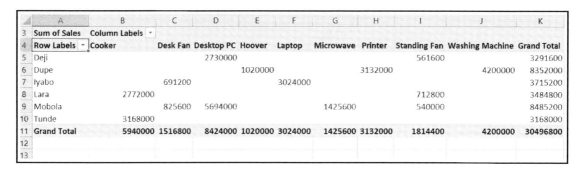

	Cooker	Desk Fan	Desktop PC	Hoover	Laptop	Microwave	Printer	Standing Fan	Washing Machine	Grand Total
Sum of Sales	Column Labels									
Row Labels	Cooker	Desk Fan	Desktop PC	Hoover	Laptop	Microwave	Printer	Standing Fan	Washing Machine	Grand Total
Deji			2730000					561600		3291600
Dupe				1020000			3132000		4200000	8352000
Iyabo		691200			3024000					3715200
Lara	2772000							712800		3484800
Mobola		825600	5694000			1425600		540000		8485200
Tunde	3168000									3168000
Grand Total	5940000	1516800	8424000	1020000	3024000	1425600	3132000	1814400	4200000	30496800

Doing that results in this:

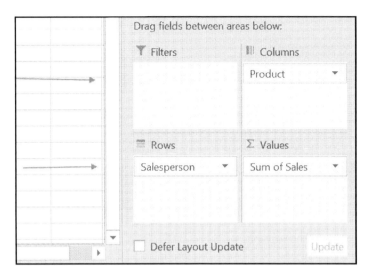

Another variation to the layout is to show sales by product, then show the salesperson as a filter:

	A	B
1	Salesperson	(All)
2		
3	**Row Labels**	**Sum of Sales**
4	Cooker	5,940,000
5	Desk Fan	1,516,800
6	Desktop PC	8,424,000
7	Hoover	1,020,000
8	Laptop	3,024,000
9	Microwave	1,425,600
10	Printer	3,132,000
11	Standing Fan	1,814,400
12	Washing Machine	4,200,000
13	**Grand Total**	**30,496,800**
14		

This results in the following:

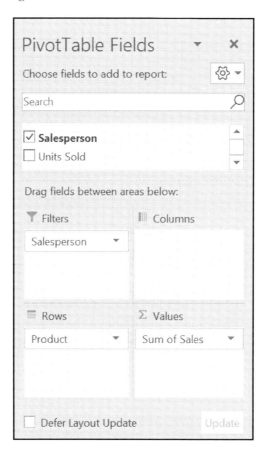

By clicking the drop-down arrow beside the `Salesperson (All)` filter, you can selectively display the results for any of the salespersons, any combination of them, or all of the salespersons.

Apart from showing the sales totals, you can also show sales as a percentage of the overall total or of average sales. In this way, you can show the contribution of a product or salesperson to the overall sales.

The following screenshot shows product sales in total and as percentages of gross sales. In order to achieve this, simply drag the `Sales` field to the **Values** box again so that it now appears twice. Right-click on the `Sum of Sales 2` column to reveal a drop-down menu, then select **Show Values**, and then finally select **Grand Total** from the second menu that appears. An illustration of product sales in total and as percentages of gross sales is shown in the following screenshot:

	A	B	C	D	E	F	G	H
1								
2								
3	Row Labels	Sum of Sales	Percentage		Row Labels	Sum of Sales	Percentage	
4	Cooker	5940000	19.48%		Deji	3291600	10.79%	
5	Desk Fan	1516800	4.97%		Dupe	8352000	27.39%	
6	Desktop PC	8424000	27.62%		Iyabo	3715200	12.18%	
7	Hoover	1020000	3.34%		Lara	3484800	11.43%	
8	Laptop	3024000	9.92%		Mobola	8485200	27.82%	
9	Microwave	1425600	4.67%		Tunde	3168000	10.39%	
10	Printer	3132000	10.27%		**Grand Total**	**30496800**	**100.00%**	
11	Standing Fan	1814400	5.95%					
12	Washing Machine	4200000	13.77%					
13	**Grand Total**	**30496800**	**100.00%**					
14								
15								
16								

The previous table shows sales by salespersons and as percentages of gross sales. This is actually a second pivot table that uses the same range but using the table on cell `E3` of the sheet housing the original pivot table. The **Show Values as...** menu has a wide range of options demonstrating the flexibility of pivot tables.

If, in trying out the various options, you mess up your table, you can simply discard it and create another one. Hopefully, this time, you would have learned from your mistakes and shifted up a notch in your experience of creating and working with pivot tables. Sometimes, people understand reports better when they are supported by diagrams and charts.

To create a pivot chart, select your pivot table, select **Analyze** from the pivot table tools context-sensitive menu, then select **Pivot Chart**. A wide range of chart types will be displayed. Select one and a pivot chart appears beside your pivot table:

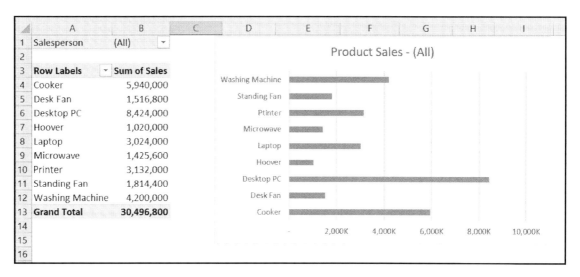

The chart is dynamic so that if you filter your table to reflect, say, one salesperson, `Iyabo`, the chart automatically updates to reflect only Iyabo's results. This screenshot shows a pivot table and a pivot chart that have been filtered to show just Iyabo's sales:

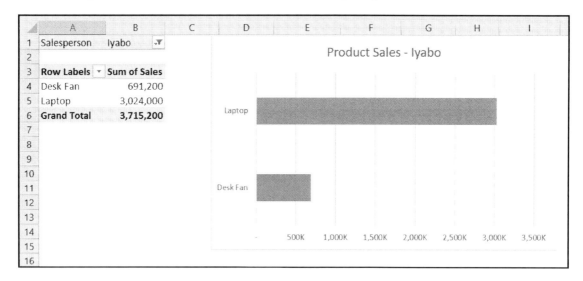

Implementing pivot tables

In the `Marks.xlsx` file, we have the percentages of all of the students. Now, let's say we want to find out who the top 10 students are, so that we can award them during our class function. Enter the pivot table using the following steps:

1. Navigate to the `Top scores` worksheet in the file, which contains all of the students and their percentages in a table.
2. Now, to create a pivot table, we will select all of the columns in the table and create a pivot table using the **PivotTable** option in the menu:

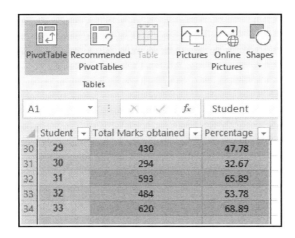

This results in the following table:

Row Labels ▾	Sum of Total Marks obtained	Sum of Percentage
1	479	53.22222222
10	407	45.22222222
11	491	54.55555556
12	546	60.66666667
13	400	44.44444444
14	463	51.44444444
15	493	54.77777778
16	513	57
17	428	47.55555556
18	541	60.11111111
19	459	51

PivotTable Fields

Choose fields to add to report:

Search

☑ Student
☑ Total Marks obtained
☑ Percentage

More Tables...

3. Since we want to find out the top 10 scores, we can use a built-in filter in the **PivotTable** filters. To reveal the following drop-down list, click on the filter icon in the corner of the **Row Labels** column:

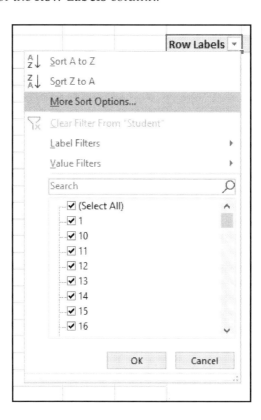

4. Navigate to **Value filters** and select the **Top 10...** option from there, as follows:

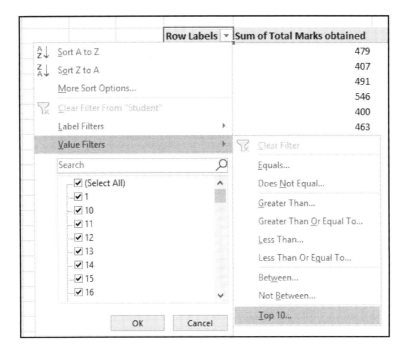

This reveals the following window:

Here, you can choose how many values you want to display, from which column you want to filter the top 10, and many more options.

5. Make sure that everything in the window looks similar to the preceding screenshot and click on **OK**. Doing so leads to the following output:

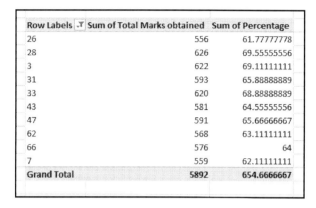

Row Labels	Sum of Total Marks obtained	Sum of Percentage
26	556	61.77777778
28	626	69.55555556
3	622	69.11111111
31	593	65.88888889
33	620	68.88888889
43	581	64.55555556
47	591	65.66666667
62	568	63.11111111
66	576	64
7	559	62.11111111
Grand Total	**5892**	**654.6666667**

As seen here, we can see the students who scored the highest grades. But we need them in descending order of their percentages, so that the highest scorer is displayed first.

6. For this, we will again click on the filter icon and navigate to **More Sort Options...**, as shown here:

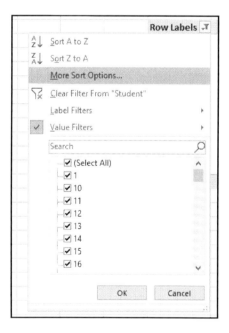

This results in the following window:

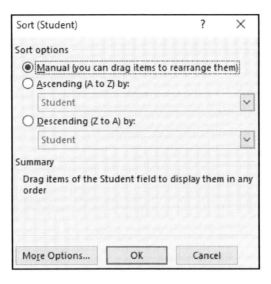

7. Here, we will now sort the students into descending order, based on the **sum of percentages**, as shown here:

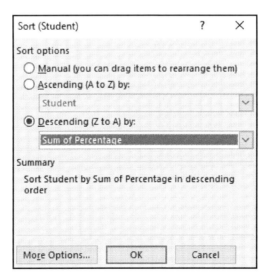

This results in the following output:

Row Labels ⬇T	Sum of Total Marks obtained	Sum of Percentage
28	626	69.55555556
3	622	69.11111111
33	620	68.88888889
31	593	65.88888889
47	591	65.66666667
43	581	64.55555556
66	576	64
62	568	63.11111111
7	559	62.11111111
26	556	61.77777778
Grand Total	**5892**	**654.6666667**

Hence, we have the results of the top 10 students in the class! This shows how powerful a pivot table can be when used right.

Pitfalls to avoid

In constructing your formulas, it is easy to get carried away and, very soon, the formula becomes very complex and unfriendly. While it is desirable to keep formulas compact, they should be simple and easy for a third party to follow. If necessary, break up the formula into two or more parts so that it becomes easier to follow while retaining the original effect.

Alternatively, you can use *Alt + Enter* to force part of the formula to the next line. This will not affect the result of the formula, but it will make the formula easier to understand. Consider the following example:

```
=INDEX(C5:G10,MATCH(J20,C5:C10,0),MATCH(K19,C5:G5,0))
```

This complex formula can be broken down to three parts with the use of *Alt + Enter*, as follows:

```
=INDEX(C5:G10,
MATCH(J20,C5:C10,0),
MATCH(K19,C5:G5,0))
```

As we can see, this makes it easier to decipher.

Protect sheets

If you are going to share your model with others, it is important that you protect your formulas against inadvertent modifications that can render the model useless. In order to do this, first highlight the cells without formulas that you want to modify, press *Ctrl + 1* to open the **Format Cells** dialog box, go to the **Protection** tab, check **Locked**, and click **OK**. This will unlock the cells that may be modified.

Now, go to the **Review** tab, then select **Protect Sheet**. The **Protect Sheet** dialog box appears. Enter a password to unprotect it if desired, then click **OK**. Now, the cells with formulas, which are protected, can only be viewed but not modified. You should enter a particular value only once. If you need to enter the same value in another location, simply refer to the original cell where the first entry was made. Any subsequent occurrences of the same value should also refer to the original entry rather than to any of the secondary cells containing the same value.

For example, an interest rate of 15% is first entered on sheet 1, cell **B5**. If interest is required in sheet 2, cell **D16**, rather than typing 15% again, you simply refer to sheet 1, cell **B5**, by typing =, then entering sheet 1, cell **B5**. If interest appears again on sheet 3, cell **J13**, theoretically, you could refer to sheet 2, cell **D16**. However, in order to preserve a simple audit trail, the reference should be to the original entry of that value, sheet 1, cell **B5**. Try and use only one formula per row.

Use your knowledge of relative, absolute, and mixed cell referencing to construct your formulas so that you can enter it in one cell, then copy or fill the formulas across the other years. The fewer times you have to enter a formula, the lower the chances of making a mistake are.

Summary

In this chapter, we learned about the power of formulas and functions and how we can use them to speed up our modeling and make it more interesting. We also worked through examples of some of the more common functions such as the VLOOKUP, MATCH, and CHOOSE functions.

In the next chapter, we will look at one of the features that forms the backbone of Excel—the referencing framework. Understanding this framework and knowing how to apply its principles will help you to speed up your work and improve your productivity.

4

Applying the Referencing Framework in Excel

Let's assume that a worksheet in Microsoft Excel is divided into over 1 million rows and over 16,000 columns. The rows are labeled **1**, **2**, **3**, and so on, up to **1,048,576**, and the columns are labeled **A**, **B**, **C**, and so on, up to **XFD**. The rows and columns intersect to form over 16 billion cells in one worksheet.

However, since a cell is identified by the columns and rows that intersect to form it, each cell has a unique identification, which is conventionally written as the intersecting column and row names. Thus, the **UV** column and row **59** form the **UV59** cell. There is no other **UV59** cell on that worksheet, of that workbook, on that computer. This feature forms the basis for the referencing framework in Excel. This chapter will talk about the various types of referencing frameworks and how to implement each one of them in order to simplify vast collections of data.

In this chapter, we will cover the following topics:

- Introduction to the framework
- Relative referencing
- Absolute referencing
- Mixed referencing
- Implementing the referencing framework

Introduction to the framework

The referencing framework ensures that you can use the contents of any cell simply by including its cell reference in a formula. The following screenshot is the simplest example of this. By typing =D4 in cell **F5**, the contents of cell **D4**, Happy day, have been duplicated in cell **F5**:

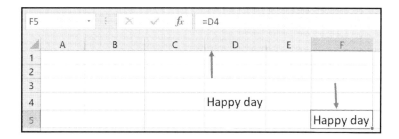

You can enter a formula in Excel by typing the values for each part of the formula directly into the cell, as shown in the following screenshot:

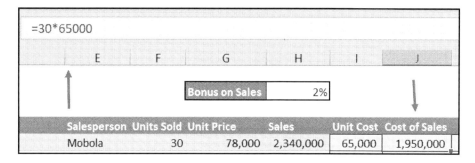

Cost of Sales is Units Sold × Unit Cost, which in this case is 30 × 65,000. The formula bar shows that we entered =30*65000 to get 1,950,000.

The two major shortcomings of this method are as follows:

- It isn't clear where the figures have come from. Several months down the line, when you come to review your model, you don't want to have to think through the whole process again in order to determine the source of the input.
- If the cells containing the values you have entered need to be modified in order to accommodate new and/or more accurate information, wherever those variables occur or have been used in formulas in your model, you would need to go and update them one by one accordingly.

Relative referencing

To avoid the aforementioned shortcomings, you should enter the cell references of the cells containing the values, rather than typing the actual values, as shown in the following screenshot:

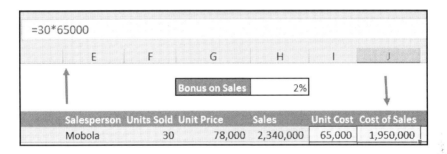

The formula bar in the preceding screenshot shows that we entered F5*I5.

In this way, it is clear where the input is coming from. All the cells that have formulas that refer to those cells will be automatically updated.

Another advantage of referencing is that, by default, Excel registers the position of the cell references relative to the active cell. So, in the preceding example, **F5** is registered as four cells to the left, and **I5** is registered as one cell to the left of the active cell, **J5**.

The relevance of this is that, when you copy that formula to another location, Excel remembers the positions of the original cell references included in the formula, relative to the original active cell. Excel then adjusts the references accordingly in order to maintain those positions relative to the new active cell.

So, if the formula is copied 15 cells down, the row part of the reference is adjusted by 15 rows down, and so `F5*I5` automatically becomes `F20*I20`. In this way, since the formula is the same, that is, `Units Sold × Unit Cost`, we can simply copy our formula down the list and still obtain the correct answers. This can be seen in the following screenshot:

=F20*I20

D	E	F	G	H	I	J	K
			Bonus on Sales	2%			
	Salesperson	Units Sold	Unit Price	Sales	Unit Cost	Cost of Sales	Commission
	Mobola	30	78,000	2,340,000	65,000	1,950,000	
	Iyabo	36	19,200	691,200	16,000	576,000	
	Dupe	27	54,000	1,458,000	45,000	1,215,000	
	Mobola	44	32,400	1,425,600	27,000	1,188,000	
	Deji	26	21,600	561,600	18,000	468,000	
	Deji	35	78,000	2,730,000	65,000	2,275,000	
	Lara	42	66,000	2,772,000	55,000	2,310,000	
	Tunde	48	66,000	3,168,000	55,000	2,640,000	
	Mobola	43	19,200	825,600	16,000	688,000	
	Dupe	31	54,000	1,674,000	45,000	1,395,000	
	Mobola	25	21,600	540,000	18,000	450,000	
	Mobola	43	78,000	3,354,000	65,000	2,795,000	
	Dupe	50	84,000	4,200,000	70,000	3,500,000	
	Iyabo	36	84,000	3,024,000	70,000	2,520,000	
	Lara	33	21,600	712,800	18,000	594,000	
	Dupe	34	30,000	1,020,000	25,000	850,000	

This wouldn't work in the example we saw in the previous section, where we entered the values directly into the active cell. If we copied down in that case, we would get the same value, `1,950,000`, all the way down the list.

This technique of referencing the cells, instead of their actual values, is called relative referencing.

There are several different ways to copy to a range of cells, which are as follows:

- The first way is to select the cell or range of cells to be copied, press *Ctrl + C*, select the range of cells to which you are going to copy, and then press *Enter* or *Ctrl + V*.

If you press *Ctrl + V*, Excel places a *Ctrl* icon at the bottom right of the last cell of the range. You can then click on the icon or simply press *Ctrl* and a box of **Paste Special** options will appear, as shown in the following screenshot:

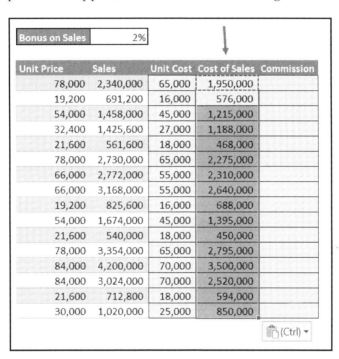

Bonus on Sales	2%			
Unit Price	Sales	Unit Cost	Cost of Sales	Commission
78,000	2,340,000	65,000	1,950,000	
19,200	691,200	16,000	576,000	
54,000	1,458,000	45,000	1,215,000	
32,400	1,425,600	27,000	1,188,000	
21,600	561,600	18,000	468,000	
78,000	2,730,000	65,000	2,275,000	
66,000	2,772,000	55,000	2,310,000	
66,000	3,168,000	55,000	2,640,000	
19,200	825,600	16,000	688,000	
54,000	1,674,000	45,000	1,395,000	
21,600	540,000	18,000	450,000	
78,000	3,354,000	65,000	2,795,000	
84,000	4,200,000	70,000	3,500,000	
84,000	3,024,000	70,000	2,520,000	
21,600	712,800	18,000	594,000	
30,000	1,020,000	25,000	850,000	

You can then select, paste format, paste values, transpose, or perform any one of the other options.

This feature isn't available if you press *Enter* to paste.

- The second way is built into Excel. There is a small black box that appears at the bottom right of the selected cell, called the **fill handle**. When you hover the cursor over the fill handle, it turns into a thick black cross. Select the cell with the value to be copied, and then hold the right mouse button down on the fill handle and drag it down the range of cells that you want to copy. Then, release the right mouse button. The following screenshot shows the fill handle of a cell in Excel:

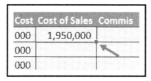

- Alternatively, you could just double-click on the fill handle and all the cells below, up to the last row of the table. These will be filled by the original cell. You don't need to preselect the cells—all you need to do is press *Ctrl + C* for this method to work.

  However, the cells in the adjacent column, left or right, must be populated in order to indicate to Excel how far down you wish to fill the formula.

- The last way to do this is as follows—starting with and including the cell with the formula to be copied, select the range of cells to be copied to, and then press *Ctrl + D*. All the cells that are selected will be populated with the formula. This method is my personal favorite and, along with double-clicking the fill handle, is the most elegant way to copy to a range of cells. You could also use this method to fill to the right by pressing *Ctrl + R*. You will find this very useful for filling formulas to the right, across the columns of the forecast years in your financial model.

Absolute referencing

Sometimes, you will have a formula that contains a reference that you don't want Excel to modify when you copy the formula. For example, let's say we want to calculate commission on sales for each salesperson. This would be `Sales × Commission`.

As we move down the list, the row number changes so that the reference to the sales that are made by the salespersons moves from **H5** to **H6**, to **H7**, and eventually to **H20**, which is the last record in our list.

However, the same commission percentage, which is in cell **H2**, applies to all salespersons. Thus, when we copy down the list, we need to retain the cell reference, **H2**, and so we need to lock the cell reference or make it absolute.

We do this by putting the $ sign before the column and row parts of the reference. By doing this, H2 becomes $H$2.

Instead of typing them in, Excel allows you to press the *F4* key to put the $ signs before the column and row references.

As you enter the formula, once you point to cell **H2** and it has registered in your formula, simply press the *F4* key and the dollar signs will appear, one before the H and one before the 2 to give $H$2. We will examine this in more detail via the following screenshots. The first screenshot shows the formula as it references H2:

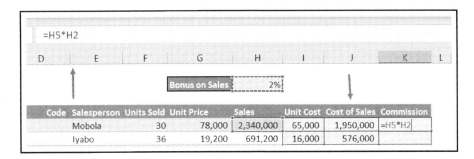

The following screenshot shows the same formula after you press *F4*:

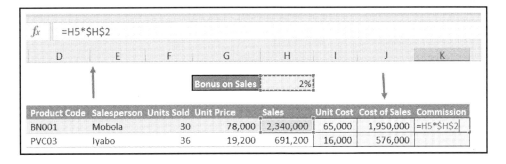

In the following screenshot, we can see that the formula has been entered in cell **K5** as `=H5*$H$2`, which becomes `46,800` when you press *Enter*:

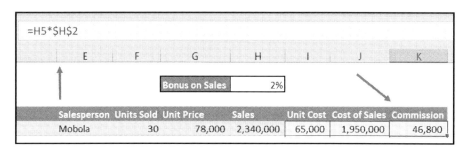

This means that when we copy the formula down the list from one row to the next, the reference to `Sales` will change accordingly, but the reference to `Commission` will be locked on cell **H2**.

The following screenshot shows the `Commission` on `Sales` for all salespersons:

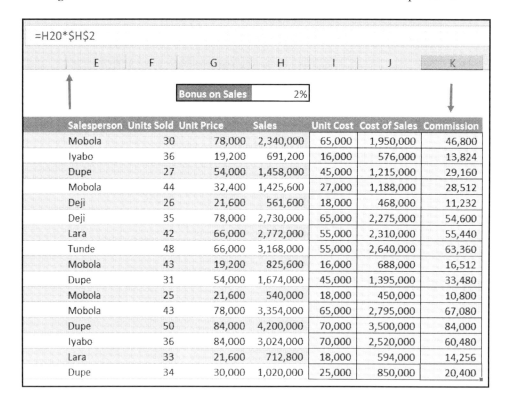

This is an example of absolute referencing.

As we mentioned previously, a cell reference is made up of the rows and columns that intersect to form that cell. Thus, if a cell is in column **G**, row **59**, its cell reference is **G59**; **G** being the column part and **59** being the row part of the cell reference. No two cells can have the same cell reference.

Mixed referencing occurs when you need to lock either the column part only, when you leave the row part of the reference relative, or lock the row part only, when you leave the column part of the reference relative. This is demonstrated in the following example in the *Mixed referencing* section.

You should take note of two things—first, that the referencing framework is only relevant when you want to copy a formula to another location. Second, its main function makes it possible for you to enter a formula once, and then copy it over a range that contains cells with formulas that have cell references with a similar positioning that's relative to the active cells.

While this framework allows you to save copious amounts of valuable time, it isn't mandatory, and if you find that you are struggling to understand this framework, you can ignore it and copy the formula manually down the list.

Mixed referencing

The following example, which is using the same `Sales Report` worksheet, seeks to compare sales that are obtained by using `MarkUps` of 15%, 20%, and 25%.

In this case, the sales is calculated as `Cost of Sales` × (1+`MarkUp` %). This is a screenshot of the layout for the markup:

H	I	J	K
	MarkUp %		
Cost of Sales	15%	20%	25%
1,950,000			
576,000			

Mixed referencing is required when you need to lock a reference in one direction only, either down **or** across to the right, but not both. In the following example, you will create the formula in cell I5, and then copy it down through rows **6** to **20** and across columns **J** and **K**. The following screenshot shows the calculation of 15% MarkUp:

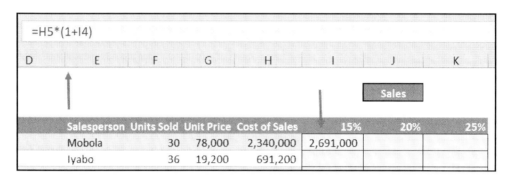

The base formula is H5*(1+I4).

Note that there are two cell references in the formula, H5 and I4, which you will need to consider individually.

Cell **H5** is the Cost of Sales. The column part is **H**, which we will look at when we consider copying to the right, across columns. The row part is **5**, which we will look at when we consider copying down the rows. When copying the formula down the rows, you want the cost of sales to change from one record to the next one down. In other words, the row part of the reference, **5**, shouldn't be locked—it should remain relative; that is, there shouldn't be a $ sign in front of it.

When copying the formula across the columns, the cost of sales remains the same as you move from one MarkUp % to the next. In other words, the column part of the reference, **H**, should be locked with a $ sign in front of it.

The following screenshot shows how to work out the referencing pattern of the first reference:

F	G	H	I	J	K
				MarkUp %	
Sold Unit Cost	Cost of Sales		15%	20%	25%
30	65,000	1,950,000	=$H5*(1+I$4)		
36	16,000	576,000			
27	45,000	1,215,000	Copying down, allow row reference to move (5).		
44	27,000	1,188,000	Copying across, lock column reference ($H)		
26	18,000	468,000			
35	65,000	2,275,000	To give - $H5		
42	55,000	2,310,000			
48	55,000	2,640,000			
43	16,000	688,000			
31	45,000	1,395,000			
25	18,000	450,000			
43	65,000	2,795,000			
50	70,000	3,500,000			
36	70,000	2,520,000			
33	18,000	594,000			
34	25,000	850,000			

Thus, our first reference is $H5.

Cell I4 is MarkUp %, which is 15%. The column part is **I**, which we will look at when we consider copying to the right across columns. The row part is **4**, which we will look at when we consider copying down the rows.

When copying the formula down the rows, you want the markup margin, which is 15%, to remain the same from one record to the next one down. In other words, the row part of the reference, 4, should be locked, and should have a $ sign in front of it. When copying the formula across the columns, the markup should move from 15% to 20%, and so on. In other words, the column part of the reference, **I**, should be locked with a $ sign in front of it.

The following screenshot shows how to work out the referencing pattern of the second reference:

	Cost	Cost of Sales	15%	20%	25%
			MarkUp %		
	65,000	1,950,000	=$H5*(1+I$4)		
	16,000	576,000			
	45,000	1,215,000		Copying down, lock row reference ($4).	
	27,000	1,188,000		Copying across, allow column reference	
	18,000	468,000		to move (I)	
	65,000	2,275,000			
	55,000	2,310,000		To give – I$4	
	55,000	2,640,000			
	16,000	688,000			
	45,000	1,395,000			
	18,000	450,000			
	65,000	2,795,000			
	70,000	3,500,000			
	70,000	2,520,000			
	18,000	594,000			
	25,000	850,000			

(Columns G, H, I, J, K)

Thus, our second reference will be I$4 and the formula would then be =$H5*(1+I$4). This results in the following output:

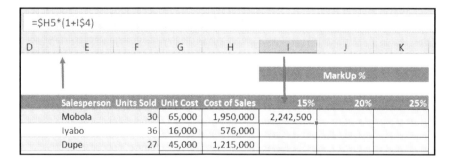

```
=$H5*(1+I$4)
```

Salesperson	Units Sold	Unit Cost	Cost of Sales	15%	20%	25%
				MarkUp %		
Mobola	30	65,000	1,950,000	2,242,500		
Iyabo	36	16,000	576,000			
Dupe	27	45,000	1,215,000			

We will now do this for all the cells.

The *F4* key on your keyboard is a toggle key that cycles through four options. Using the cell reference H5 as an example, pressing the *F4* key once will put the $ sign before both the column and row parts to give $H$5. A second press will put the $ sign in front of the row part only to give H$5. A third press will put the $ sign in front of the column part only to give $H5. Finally, a fourth press on the *F4* key will return the reference to a relative reference, H5, with no $ signs.

Now, copy the formula across and down.

It is always prudent to check that the copied formula gives the correct answer. You can do this by checking the cell at the bottom right of the range that you have copied. In this case, this is cell **K20**, which correctly refers to the cells **H20** and **K4**. The following screenshot shows the check to ensure that the formula was correctly constructed:

H	I	J	K	L
		MarkUp %		
Cost of Sales	15%	20%	25%	
1,950,000	2,242,500	2,340,000	2,437,500	
576,000	662,400	691,200	720,000	
1,215,000	1,397,250	1,458,000	1,518,750	
1,188,000	1,366,200	1,425,600	1,485,000	
468,000	538,200	561,600	585,000	
2,275,000	2,616,250	2,730,000	2,843,750	
2,310,000	2,656,500	2,772,000	2,887,500	
2,640,000	3,036,000	3,168,000	3,300,000	
688,000	791,200	825,600	860,000	
1,395,000	1,604,250	1,674,000	1,743,750	
450,000	517,500	540,000	562,500	
2,795,000	3,214,250	3,354,000	3,493,750	
3,500,000	4,025,000	4,200,000	4,375,000	
2,520,000	2,898,000	3,024,000	3,150,000	
594,000	683,100	712,800	742,500	
850,000	977,500	1,020,000	=$H20*(1+K$4)	

Implementing the referencing framework

Now that you are all caught up with the theory behind each type of referencing framework and know where to use each of them, let's apply that knowledge to a real-life scenario.

Assume that you are a teacher and that you have the marks of the students in an entire class, and you need to sort and divide the data into different groups, based on the following criteria:

- Total marks scored by the student in all languages
- Total marks scored by the student in all sciences
- Overall marks scored

The referencing framework really comes into its own in such scenarios. We can sort our data using the required criteria by following these steps:

1. Open the `Marks.xlsx` file provided to you, which contains the grades of 66 students who appeared for their midterms. The data will look similar to the following screenshot:

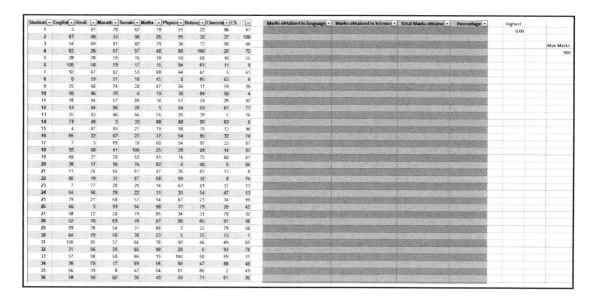

2. Now, we will start sorting the data. By looking at the first criterion, we can see that the grades for languages are present in columns **B** through **E**. So, let's input the formula for student 1 in the respective field, which in this case is **L2**. Since we want to calculate the sum of the marks, our formula will be =B2+C2+D2+E2, as shown in the following screenshot:

Student	English	Hindi	Marath	Sanskr	Maths	Physic	Botany	Chemist	CS		Marks obtained in language
1	3	97	78	62	19	55	22	96	47		=B2+C2+D2+E2
2	87	40	33	98	26	91	32	37	100		
3	54	69	81	82	79	34	73	90	60		
4	63	26	57	57	48	88	100	20	72		

This results in the following output:

	Marath	Sanskr	Maths	Physic	Botany	Chemist	CS		Marks obtained in language
1									
2	78	62	19	55	22	96	47		240

3. Now, for student 2, we can simply click the fill handle in the bottom-right corner of the sum field and drag it down to the field below it, which results in the following output:

Student	English	Hindi	Marath	Sanskr	Maths	Physic	Botany	Chemist	CS		Marks obtained in language
1	3	97	78	62	19	55	22	96	47		240
2	87	40	33	98	26	91	32	37	100		258
3	54	69	81	82	79	34	73	90	60		
4	63	26	57	57	48	88	100	20	72		

4. As we learned in the *Relative referencing* section, we can fill in all the cells with their respective values in several ways. We will use the most elegant way here, which is double-clicking the fill handle on the **L3** cell, which results in the following output:

Student	English	Hindi	Marath	Sanskr	Maths	Physic	Botany	Chemist	CS		Marks obtained in language
1	3	97	78	62	19	55	22	96	47		240
2	87	40	33	98	26	91	32	37	100		258
3	54	69	81	82	79	34	73	90	60		286
4	63	26	57	57	48	88	100	20	72		203
5	28	28	59	16	18	50	68	10	55		131
6	100	50	59	17	15	94	61	11	9		226
7	92	47	82	53	68	64	87	5	61		274
8	0	59	21	10	45	8	85	63	0		90
9	75	48	74	28	47	36	17	59	39		225
10	90	46	30	6	19	38	84	90	4		172
11	18	94	57	89	34	57	24	26	92		258
12	93	94	96	20	1	54	50	61	77		303
13	25	83	86	64	56	26	39	5	16		258
14	73	49	3	33	88	69	80	63	5		158
15	4	87	85	21	19	98	76	13	90		197
16	65	22	67	27	77	54	95	32	74		181
17	7	3	69	18	60	54	97	33	87		97
18	92	60	41	100	25	28	84	14	97		293
19	49	37	70	52	41	14	75	60	61		208
20	38	17	98	76	82	4	48	5	84		229
21	11	24	84	61	47	26	63	13	8		180
22	65	19	31	87	58	99	32	8	74		202
23	7	77	28	28	14	63	41	37	13		140
24	44	56	29	22	31	30	54	47	13		151
25	79	21	68	57	54	87	23	14	99		225
26	46	3	93	94	98	72	79	29	42		236
27	58	72	28	79	85	34	31	79	32		237
28	52	70	69	78	87	88	65	91	26		269
29	69	39	54	31	66	3	33	79	56		193
30	64	19	56	38	23	5	75	13	1		177
31	100	85	57	64	38	92	46	49	62		306
32	31	56	30	65	98	28	5	93	78		182
33	97	98	50	86	19	100	50	89	31		331
34	36	79	17	89	56	60	47	88	48		221
35	66	39	8	42	64	81	86	2	49		155
36	58	10	82	36	40	40	71	61	35		186

As we can see, all the cells have now been populated with their respective values automatically.

As an exercise, I will leave the `Marks obtained in Sciences` column blank so that you can try this out on your own.

5. Rinse and repeat for the `Total Marks obtained` column. Our final table should look similar to the following:

Student	English	Hindi	Marath	Sanskr	Maths	Physic	Botany	Chemist	CS		Marks obtained in language	Marks obtained in Science	Total Marks obtaine
1	3	97	78	62	19	55	22	96	47		240	239	479
2	87	40	33	98	26	91	32	37	100		258	286	544
3	54	69	81	82	79	34	73	90	60		286	336	622
4	63	26	57	57	48	88	100	20	72		203	328	531
5	28	28	59	16	18	50	68	10	55		131	201	332
6	100	50	59	17	15	94	61	11	9		226	190	416
7	92	47	82	53	68	64	87	5	61		274	285	559
8	0	59	21	10	45	8	85	63	0		90	201	291
9	75	48	74	28	47	36	17	59	39		225	198	423
10	90	46	30	6	19	38	84	90	4		172	235	407
11	18	94	57	89	34	57	24	26	92		258	233	491
12	93	94	96	20	1	54	50	61	77		303	243	546
13	25	83	86	64	56	26	39	5	16		258	142	400
14	73	49	3	88	69	80	63	63	5		158	305	463
15	4	87	85	21	19	98	76	13	90		197	296	493
16	65	22	67	27	77	54	95	32	74		181	332	513
17	7	3	69	18	60	54	97	33	87		97	331	428
18	92	60	41	100	25	28	84	14	97		293	248	541
19	49	37	70	52	41	14	75	60	61		208	251	459
20	38	17	98	76	82	4	48	5	84		229	223	452
21	11	24	84	61	47	26	63	13	8		180	157	337
22	65	19	31	87	58	99	32	8	74		202	271	473
23	7	77	28	28	14	63	41	37	13		140	168	308
24	44	56	29	22	31	30	54	47	13		151	175	326
25	79	21	68	57	54	87	23	14	99		225	277	502
26	46	3	93	94	98	72	79	29	42		236	320	556
27	58	72	26	79	85	34	31	79	32		237	261	498
28	52	70	69	78	87	88	65	91	26		269	357	626
29	69	39	54	31	66	3	33	79	56		193	237	430
30	64	19	56	38	23	5	75	13	1		177	117	294
31	100	85	57	64	38	92	46	49	62		306	287	593
32	31	56	30	65	98	28	5	93	78		182	302	484
33	97	98	50	86	19	50	89	89	31		331	289	620
34	36	79	17	89	56	60	47	88	48		221	299	520
35	66	39	8	42	64	81	86	2	49		155	282	437
36	58	10	82	36	40	40	71	61	35		186	247	433

Now, let's say you want to find the percentage that each student scored. We can do that by using the following formula:

$$\text{Percentage scored} = \left(\frac{\text{Total Marks}}{\text{Max Marks}}\right) \times 100$$

For this, we will apply mixed referencing.

6. First, we will create an independent cell, **T5**, in which we will input the maximum marks that a student can score (900), as shown in the following screenshot:

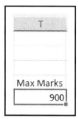

7. Now, we will input the formula to calculate the percentage for student 1 in cell **O2**, as shown here:

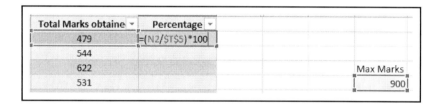

This results in the following output:

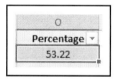

 As an exercise, use the fill handle to find the percentages for the remaining 65 students.

One more cool thing you can do here is finding the student who scored the highest grades using the =MAX() function. Once everything has been done, our final worksheet should look similar to the following screenshot:

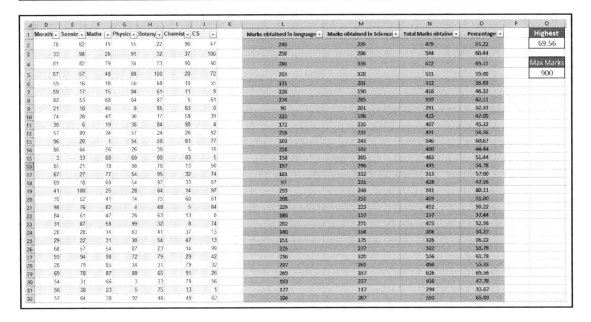

As we can see, the referencing framework in Excel has immense capabilities, all of which can be implemented in various fields.

Summary

In this chapter, we have learned about the referencing framework in Excel. We learned about the three types of referencing; that is, relative, absolute, and mixed referencing; and when to use each of them. We understood that this concept can save us a lot of time in our Excel work, but is only relevant when we need to copy a cell or range of cells containing one or more cell references to another location. We also learned about the *F4* shortcut key and how it toggles between the different forms of referencing.

In the next chapter, *Understanding the Project and Building Assumptions*, we will cover the need to understand the purpose of any project that you work on and how to build assumptions, which are necessary to project our actual results for the next three to five years.

3
Section 3: Building an Integrated Financial Model

A financial model is integrated when the various sections that define it are linked together in such a way that any alteration will ripple right through the model and update all the relevant values. This section will take you through the stages to follow when you're building your model in a systematic fashion.

This section comprises the following chapters:

- Chapter 5, *Understanding Project and Building Assumptions*
- Chapter 6, *Asset and Debt Schedules*
- Chapter 7, *Cash Flow Statement*
- Chapter 8, *Ratio Analysis*
- Chapter 9, *Valuation*
- Chapter 10, *Model Testing for Reasonableness and Accuracy*

5
Understanding Project and Building Assumptions

In financial modeling, there is no one-size-fits-all. Financial models can vary widely in size, purpose, and complexity. A valuation model is vastly different from a loan repayment model. A model that's created to expand a business will be different from one that's created to dispose of a business. A model that's created to give someone a rough idea of the value of a business will be far less complex than one that's created in support of a private placement or an initial public offering of the shares of the business. It is imperative that you understand the scope and purpose of the model you have been asked to prepare. No matter how impressive your model is, it is of no use if it doesn't meet the requirements of the user. In this chapter, you will learn how to analyze projects and learn what the purpose of a project is. You will also learn how to create assumptions to improve our project.

In this chapter, we will cover the following topics:

- Understanding the nature and purpose of a project
- Conducting interviews
- Building assumptions

Understanding the nature and purpose of a project

In order to determine the nature and purpose of a project, you will need to address a number of questions, which are as follows:

- What is the project seeking to do?
- Are you seeking to value something, project something, or both?
- What is the focus or scope of the project?

- Are you looking at the business as a whole, or a section of the business, or a particular asset, plant, or equipment?
- Who is the target audience?
- Is it for internal or personal use, or for presentation to a wider audience?
- Is it a select, knowledgeable audience or the general public?
- Is there any specialist or technical part of the project that will require you to engage an expert in that field?

The answers to each one of these questions will have an impact on how you approach your model, what type of model you build, and how detailed it is.

Conducting interviews

A significant amount of your modeling time should be allocated to discussions with the client's management. People are generally apprehensive when they're called into discussions with professionals, so you will need to allay their fears and create a non-threatening environment for your discussions. You need to make them understand that they are the experts and that you need their help to understand the business.

These interviews will help you understand why the decision was taken to prepare a financial model. They should cover the history of the company, including key policy decisions that have been taken and their impact on the company's results. You will need to make an assessment of key management personnel and the extent to which you can place reliance on their assertions. You will need to document your discussions as thoroughly as possible but prepare the client for follow-up interviews should the need arise.

Historical data

The foundation for building assumptions that we will use to forecast the company's results for the next five years is the company's historical financials. You will therefore need to obtain three or five years of the company's financial statements for this purpose. Ideally, you would want a soft copy of the accounts in Excel format. Unfortunately, what is usually available is a hard copy or a PDF file. Even when it is in Excel or CSV format, the layout will more than likely require modifications in order to bring it in line with your preferred layout.

You should therefore be prepared to type out the accounts again in Excel, in a layout that's suitable for your model. You would need to extract the balance sheets and profit and loss accounts for every year. The historical financials are extremely important since, apart from forming the basis of our assumptions and projections, they will also play a very important role when troubleshooting is required. Since we will be using the same concepts and formulas for our projected years, it helps to use a set of complete and balanced accounts as the starting point.

Building assumptions

A financial model can be defined as the collection of mathematical assumptions for the purpose of the results, financial position, and cash flow of a business in the future, often with a view to arriving at a value for the business. Building reliable assumptions is critical to the success of your model.

The following is a quick checklist for your assumptions:

- Based on actual historical figures
- Realistic
- Clearly explained
- Easily verifiable
- Properly documented
- Visually distinguishable in your model (usually with a different font) from calculated cells

General assumptions

The overall assumptions of your model are that the business will be profitable and cash flow will ultimately be positive.

You also assume that the business is a going concern (that it will be able to meet its liabilities, as they fall due, for the foreseeable future) and that information you have obtained or been given, about competitors and projected costs and revenue, is accurate.

Profit and loss and balance sheet assumptions

When you're building your financial statement assumptions, you start by identifying growth drivers. In this context, growth drivers are those indices or indicators that best capture the growth in individual items over the past three or five years.

In carrying out this exercise, you need to consider the cost-effectiveness of your decisions, particularly when dealing with items that aren't material. Sometimes, a simple best-judgement projection will be sufficient.

Profit and loss account growth drivers

Turnover is the most prominent item in a profit and loss account. It therefore makes sense to concentrate on identifying a driver for turnover and then relating some of the less significant line expenses to projected turnover.

Appropriate drivers could be year-on-year growth or inflation, or **compound annual growth rate** (**CAGR**). We will look at these two drivers now.

Year-on-year growth

This is simply the growth from one year to the next. It is usually expressed as a percentage. Year-on-year growth in turnover from **year1** to **year2** can be calculated as follows:

$$\text{Growth rate} = \frac{\text{Turnover (year2) - Turnover(year1)}}{\text{Turnover(year1)}}$$

Compound annual growth rate

To understand CAGR, you must understand the concept of compounding.

If you invest N100m (one hundred million Naira) at 10% per annum, you would expect to collect N10m in interest at the end of the year (10% of N100m). At the end of the second year, you would collect another N10m in interest, and so on. If, however, you decided not to withdraw the interest of N10m, but rather to compound it, you would have N100m + N10m = N110m to invest at 10% at the beginning of the second year. So, at the end of the second year, you would receive N11m in interest (10% of N110m). You would therefore have N110m + N11m = N121m to invest at 10% at the beginning of the third year, and so on.

The Naira is the currency of Nigeria - you can replace it with any currency of your choice and the values won't get affected!

Note that compounding over multiple years gives a higher overall return than if you withdrew the interest at the end of each year. You could also say that your N100m today is worth N110m at the end of one year and N121m at the end of 2 years, and so on. Money today is worth more tomorrow.

Year-on-year growth is seldom constant over multiple periods; it varies from year to year. In practice, you might have a scenario like the one displayed in the following screenshot:

		fx =(D4-C4)/C4				
	B	C	D	E	F	G
		Yr1	Yr2	Yr3	Yr4	Yr5
Revenue		150	280	320	350	450
Year on Year Growth			87%	14%	9%	29%

 CAGR is an index that's used to convert diverse growth rates over multiple periods into a single growth rate over all the periods.

The CAGR of an item takes the value of that item in the first year and the value in the final year and, assuming compounding, calculates a growth rate for the period.

The formula for CAGR is as follows:

$$\text{Value in year } 1 = V1;$$
$$\text{Value in year } 2 \text{ is } V2 = V1 + (V1 \times r);$$
$$\text{where } r \text{ is the CAGR}$$

We can simplify this by isolating *V1* on the right-hand side of the equation, as follows:

$$V2 = V1 \times (1 + r)$$

Thus, the value in year three is as follows:

$$V3 = V2 \times (1 + r)$$

By substituting the value of *V2* in the preceding equation, we get the following:

$$V3 = V1 \times (1 + r) \times (1 + r) = V1 \times (1 + r)^2$$

Now, *V4* is as follows:

$$V4 = V3 \times (1 + r)$$

Substituting *V3*, we get the following:

$$V4 = V1 \times (1 + r) \times (1 + r) \times (1 + r) = V1 \times (1 + r)^3$$

This leads to the following general formula:

$$V_n = V1 \times (1 + r)^{n-1}$$

We take the following steps to rearrange and make *r* the subject of the formula:

$$V1 \times (1 + r)^{n-1} = V_n$$

We move *V1* to the other side so that it becomes $V_n/V1$:

$$(1 + r)^{n-1} = \frac{V_n}{V1}$$

We move the power sign to the other side so that it becomes *1/(n-1)*:

$$1 + r = [\frac{V_n}{V1}]^{\frac{1}{n-1}}$$

Now, the CAGR is as follows:

$$r = [\frac{V_n}{V1}]^{\frac{1}{n-1}} - 1$$

When this is written out in full, it's as follows:

$$\left[\frac{\text{Value in year n}}{\text{Value in year 1}}\right]^{\frac{1}{n-1}} - 1$$

Here, n is the total number of years.

The CAGR in revenue in our example will be as follows:

$$\left[\frac{\text{Revenue in first year}}{\text{Revenue in final year}}\right]^{\frac{1}{4}} - 1$$

The power or exponent is represented by ^ in Excel. Therefore, 2^2 becomes 2^2 in Excel. We will look at the CAGR formula here:

	fx =(G4/C4)^(1/4)-1				
B	**C**	**D**	**E**	**F**	**G**
	Yr1	Yr2	Yr3	Yr4	Yr5
Revenue	150	280	320	350	450
CAGR	=(G4/C4)^(1/4)-1				

This gives us a CAGR of 32%, as shown in the following screenshot:

	fx =(G4/C4)^(1/4)-1				
B	**C**	**D**	**E**	**F**	**G**
	Yr1	Yr2	Yr3	Yr4	Yr5
Reven	150	280	320	350	450
CAGR	32%				

 Note that you can use the same formula to calculate the CAGR of other items, such as the cost of sales.

In general, we apply our growth drivers to the following values:

- **Turnover—price and volume**: For a simple model, you can base your projections on turnover. However, in order to make your model more flexible, you may wish to increase the detail or granularity of it. In such cases, you would break down the turnover into its component parts and base your projections on price and volume.
- **Purchases—cost and volume**: Similarly, for purchases and other direct expenses, if necessary, you can make your model more granular and base your projections on cost and volume.
- **Overheads**: Most overheads can be projected based on the historical percentage of turnover. Then, the average—over the previous five years—percentage of turnover will be applied to the estimated turnover for each of the next five estimated years.

Balance sheet growth drivers

Balance sheet growth drivers are not as straightforward as profit and loss drivers. While a profit and loss item is the sum of occurrences of that item within the period under review, a balance sheet item is made up of an opening balance, plus or minus movements in that item during the period, in order to arrive at a balance at a specific point in time; that is, the period end.

A wise man once said that *revenue is vanity, profit is sanity, but cash is reality*. We identify appropriate balance sheet drivers by considering cash flow.

Balance sheet items that drive cash flow are the elements of working capital—inventory, debtors, and creditors. An increase or decrease in these items has a direct effect on cash flow. The following diagram shows this process:

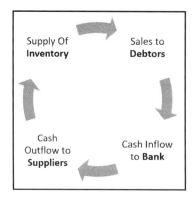

The working capital cycle consists of how quickly you turn over your stock, how quickly your debtors pay, and how quickly you pay your creditors. In general, the faster the cycle turns, the quicker its components are converted into cash. Balance sheet growth drivers are calculated using the concept of *days of....* The following diagram shows the different labels for each process:

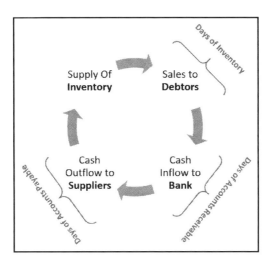

Days of inventory

The management of a company will need to ensure that they have enough stock to satisfy customers and avoid supply delays. On the other hand, they shouldn't keep too much stock, as this ties down cash that could otherwise be utilized productively.

Over time, management will learn the optimum level of stock to hold, as well as when to reorder stock, so as to strike an appropriate balance between satisfying customers and not overstocking. Once proper stock control has been achieved, the amount of time it takes before stock is sold (days of inventory) should be fairly constant and can be used as a basis for estimating future inventory.

Days of inventory or inventory days is calculated as follows:

$$\frac{\text{average inventory}...}{\text{daily cost of goods sold (COGS)}}$$

$$= \frac{\text{opening inventory} + \text{closing inventory}}{2} \div \frac{\text{annual COGS}}{365}$$

Here, **opening inventory** is the inventory at the beginning of the year, **closing inventory** is the inventory at the end of the year, and **COGS** is the cost of the goods that were sold.

Debtor days

A similar assumption holds for debtors. Once management has established an efficient debt collection process, the number of days it takes, on average, for trade debtors to pay becomes fairly constant over time and can be used to estimate future debtors.

The formula for debtor days is as follows:

$$= \frac{\frac{\text{average debtors}}{\text{daily sales}}}{\frac{\text{opening debtors} + \text{closing debtors}}{2} \div \frac{\text{annual sales}}{365}}$$

Here, **opening debtors** is the count of debtors at the beginning of the year, and **closing debtors** is the count of debtors at the end of the year.

Creditor days

Finally, once management has been able to negotiate favorable credit terms with its suppliers and an efficient payment process has been put in place, the amount of time it takes to pay suppliers becomes fairly constant.

The formula for creditor days is as follows:

$$= \frac{\frac{\text{average creditors}}{\text{daily COGS}}}{\frac{\text{opening creditors} + \text{closing creditors}}{2} \div \frac{\text{annual COGS}}{365}}$$

Here, **opening creditors** is the count of creditors at the beginning of the year and **closing creditors** is the count of creditors at the end of the year.

Once we have established our historical growth drivers, we turn to our notes from discussions with management and our own assessments in order to create assumptions of the projected behavior of the selected items and balances over the next five years.

For profit and loss items, we will be looking out for phrases such as ...*x should increase by historic CAGR over the next five years*, or... *should increase by 0.5% more (or less) than historic CAGR*, or... *should show a gradual increase from y% to z% over the next five years*, or ...*will stay the same for the next two years, then increase gradually to y% in the fifth year.*

Continuing with our example, say the sales manager projects that turnover will increase by 2% less than the historical CAGR over the next five years, we would proceed as follows.

Using your knowledge of the referencing framework in Excel, you would highlight all the cells for the projected years to be populated with the growth driver, CAGR<2% (cells **H4** to **L4**), construct your formula for CAGR using the appropriate absolute and relative referencing, and subtract 2%:

```
CAGR = ($G$4/$C$4)^(1/4)-1-2%
```

Then, press *Ctrl + Enter*. This will give you the projected growth drivers for the next five years, as shown in the following diagram:

Next, we apply the growth to the turnover of the last year with actual results, Yr5A (the **A** stands for **actual**), to get the turnover for the first year of estimated figures, Yr6E (the **E** stands for **estimate**), using the following formula:

```
=G4*(1+H5)
```

We will repeat this for Yr7E and each subsequent projected year.

In practice, you would highlight cells **H4** to **L4**, type the formula once, and then press *Ctrl + Enter* to populate all the highlighted cells at once, as follows:

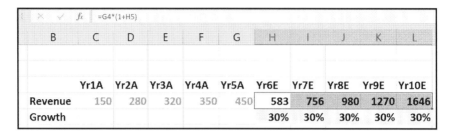

Apply the same procedure to other major profit and loss items.

For less significant profit and loss items, such as `Sales and distribution`, you first calculate the percentage turnover for each of the historical years.

The following screenshot shows overheads as a percentage of turnover:

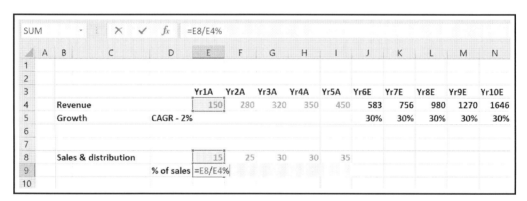

You would then project this driver forward as the average of the five historical years.

Note that the quickest way to populate a range of cells with the same formula is to do the following:

1. Select the range of cells.
2. Construct the formula using relative, absolute, and mixed referencing as appropriate (see `Chapter 4`, *Applying the Referencing Framework in Excel*, for more information).
3. Hold down *Ctrl*, and then press *Enter* (*Ctrl + Enter*).

All the cells in the range will be filled with the same formula as if you had copied the formula to each of them.

If you forget step 1 and fail to select the range of cells before constructing the formula, all is not lost:

1. Construct the formula using relative, absolute, and mixed referencing as appropriate (see Chapter 4, *Applying the Referencing Framework in Excel*, for more information).
2. Select the range of cells to be populated with the formula, starting with and including the cell in which you have typed the formula.
3. Now, press *Ctrl + D* if the range of cells is downwards or *Ctrl + R* if the range of cells is to the right.

The following screenshot shows how to calculate the growth drivers to be used over the five forecasted years:

Finally, you would apply the projected drivers to each of the estimated years, Yr6E to Yr10E.

The following screenshot shows grossing up the expense by applying the growth driver to last year's value:

	J9	▾	⋮	✕	✓	ƒx	=J4*J9						
	A	B	C	D	E	F	G	H	I	J	K	L	M	N
1														
2														
3					Yr1A	Yr2A	Yr3A	Yr4A	Yr5A	Yr6E	Yr7E	Yr8E	Yr9E	Yr10E
4		Revenue			150	280	320	350	450	583	756	980	1270	1646
5		Growth		CAGR - 2%						30%	30%	30%	30%	30%
6														
7														
8		Sales & distribution			15	25	30	30	35	=J4*J9				
9				% of sales	10.0%	8.9%	9.4%	8.6%	7.8%	8.9%	8.9%	8.9%	8.9%	8.9%
10														

By doing this, you will arrive at the projected sales and distribution costs for Yr6E to Yr10E.

The following screenshot shows filling the other forecast years with the same formula:

	J8	▾	⋮	✕	✓	ƒx	=J4*J9						
	A	B	C	D	E	F	G	H	I	J	K	L	M	N
1														
2														
3					Yr1A	Yr2A	Yr3A	Yr4A	Yr5A	Yr6E	Yr7E	Yr8E	Yr9E	Yr10E
4		Revenue			150	280	320	350	450	583	756	980	1270	1646
5		Growth		CAGR - 2%						30%	30%	30%	30%	30%
6														
7														
8		Sales & distribution			15	25	30	30	35	52	68	87	113	147
9				% of sales	10.0%	8.9%	9.4%	8.6%	7.8%	8.9%	8.9%	8.9%	8.9%	8.9%

In this way, you would build up your profit and loss account for the projected/estimated years, `Yr6E` to `Yr10E`. At this stage, your profit and loss account would be complete, except for depreciation and interest.

For balance sheet items, we will need to revisit our formulas for *days of…*:

$$\text{Days of inventory} = \frac{\text{average inventory…}}{\text{daily COGS}}$$

Rearranging the formula, we get the following:

$$\text{average inventory} = \text{days of inventory} \times \text{daily COGS}$$

Let's expand on average inventory and daily cost of goods sold:

$$\frac{\text{opening inventory} + \text{closing inventory}}{2} = \text{days of inventory} \times \frac{\text{annual COGS}}{365}$$

Then, by rearranging the formula again, we get the following:

$$\text{closing inventory} = 2 \times \text{days of inventory} \times \frac{\text{annual COGS}}{365} - \text{closing inventory}$$

Days of inventory: We have mentioned that days of inventory is expected to be stable over the years. You could therefore take the average of historical days of inventory over the past five years and use this as the projected driver for inventory over the next five years. If there have been any occurrences that indicate that activity may be affected in such a way as to have a significant effect on COGS, you could apply a best-judgement adjustment to the average days of inventory calculated. For example, a big competitor entering into the market could result in a temporary slowdown in sales, thereby leading to a reduction in COGS and thus an increase in days of inventory.

Opening inventory: The opening inventory of one year is the closing inventory for the previous year. So, the opening inventory for `Yr6E` is the closing inventory from `Yr5A`.

Annual COGS: This will have been calculated earlier in the projection and be built up of your profit and loss account for `Yr6E` to `Yr10E`. Since all the items on the right of the equation are known, we can calculate the closing inventory for `Yr6E` and then repeat the procedure for `Yr7E` to `Yr10E`. The following screenshot show the computation of inventory for the projected years:

				Yr1A	Yr2A	Yr3A	Yr4A	Yr5A
					=AVERAGE(E28:F28)/(F23/365)			
14	**Balance Sheet Assumptions**							
15	**Key Ratios (Days of...)**							
16	Inventories (Daily cost of sales)				=AVERAGE(E28:F28)/(F23/365)			
17	Trade and other receivables (Daily sales)							
18	Trade and other payables (Daily cost of sales)							
19								
20	**PROFIT & LOSS**							
21								
22	Revenue			260,810	272,241	245,009	297,938	311,453
23	Cost of sales			177,782	181,657	186,876	193,989	200,786
24	GROSS PROFIT			83,028	90,584	58,133	103,949	110,667
25								
26	**BALANCE SHEET**							
27								
28	Inventories			15,545	18,007	21,731	14,530	21,860
29	Trade and other receivables			20,864	31,568	35,901	33,812	39,063
30	Cash and cash equivalents			7,459	17,252	9,265	65,106	67,707
31	**Total current assets**			43,868	66,827	66,897	113,447	128,630

Debtor days: In the same way, debtor days can be represented as follows:

$$\text{closing debtors} = 2 \times \text{days of debtors} \times \frac{\text{annual turnover}}{365} - \text{opening debtors}$$

The average of the historical debtor days will be taken as projected debtor days for `Yr6E` to `Yr10E`.

The following screenshot shows the computation of debtors for the projected years:

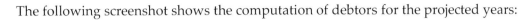

	C	D	E	F	G	H	I
SUM			=AVERAGE(E28:F28)/(F22/365)				
1			Yr1A	Yr2A	Yr3A	Yr4A	Yr5A
14 Balance Sheet Assumptions							
15 Key Ratios (Days of...)							
16 Inventories (Daily cost of sales)				34	39	34	33
17 Trade and other receivables (Daily sales)				=AVERAGE(E28:F28)/(F22/365)			
18 Trade and other payables (Daily cost of sales)							
19							
20 PROFIT & LOSS							
21							
22 Revenue			260,810	272,241	245,009	297,938	311,453
23 Cost of sales			177,782	181,657	186,876	193,989	200,786
24 GROSS PROFIT			83,028	90,584	58,133	103,949	110,667
25							
26 BALANCE SHEET							
27							
28 Inventories			15,545	18,007	21,731	14,530	21,860
29 Trade and other receivables			20,864	31,568	35,901	33,812	39,063
30 Cash and cash equivalents			7,459	17,252	9,265	65,106	67,707
31 Total current assets			43,868	66,827	66,897	113,447	128,630

Creditor days: Finally, we have the following equation:

$$\text{closing creditors} = 2 \times \text{days of creditors} \times \frac{\text{annual COGS}}{365} - \text{opening creditors}$$

The average of the historical creditor days will be used to estimate creditor days for `Yr6E` to `Yr10E`.

The following screenshot shows the computation of creditors for the projected years:

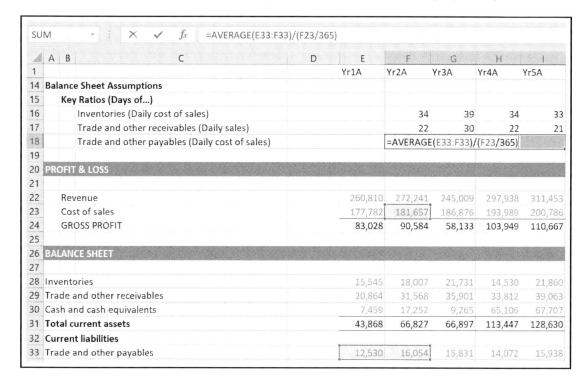

Once we have populated the balance sheet with these items, we will have a complete balance sheet, except for long-term assets, loans, and, of course, cash.

Summary

In this chapter, we have seen that without thorough knowledge of the nature and purpose of a project, you could end up with a model that doesn't meet the specifications of your client. We have learned about the nature of and reason for assumptions, as well as the importance of discussions with management in projecting your assumptions into the future. In making our assumptions, we have realized the importance of historical financials, balance sheets, profit and loss accounts, and cash flow statements. We have also learned about historical financials, which are an essential starting point in resolving anomalies that may arise in our model.

In the next chapter, *Asset and Debt Schedules*, we will learn how to project long-term assets and borrowings. We will be introduced to different approaches: a complex but more accurate method, and a simple, more subjective approach. We will also learn how to update the balance sheet and profit and loss with output from our asset and debt schedules.

6
Asset and Debt Schedules

At this stage, the projected balance sheet and profit and loss accounts are complete except for the effects of **capital expenditure** (**CapEx**)—purchase, disposal and depreciation, long-term debt, fresh issues, repayments, and interest charges. The fixed asset, depreciation, and debt schedules are very important to our model as they tend to appear as very significant amounts in financial statements. These are long-term balances and are not covered by growth drivers. You will rely on the client to give you information about their plans for CapEx and debt for over the next five years. If you have no information on this, you will generally assume that the existing balances will continue to be serviced for the duration of the projected years, or until they are fully written down or off—whichever comes first.

This chapter covers the following topics:

- Understanding the BASE and corkscrew concepts
- Approaches to modeling assets
- Asset schedule
- Debt schedule
- Creating a loan amortization schedule

Understanding the BASE and corkscrew concepts

These are common standards to follow in modeling our balance sheet items. **BASE** is an acronym that stands for **beginning add additions less subtractions equals end**. The corkscrew concept refers to the way in which the base setup is connected from one period to the next. In the following screenshot, we will see that the closing balance from one year is carried forward as the opening balance of the next year:

C	D	E	F	G
		Yr1A	Yr2A	Yr3A
Opening		100,000	109,000	134,000
Additions		34,000	60,000	15,000
Disposals		(25,000)	(35,000)	(20,000)
Closing		109,000	134,000	129,000

We notice that the movement is from the opening balance, which goes down the rows of the first year to the closing balance, then back up to the opening balance of the second year, then down the rows of the second year, and so on. This creates a corkscrew effect, as seen in the following screenshot:

C	D	E	F	G
		Yr1A	Yr2A	Yr3A
Opening		100,000	109,000	134,000
Additions		34,000	60,000	15,000
Disposals		(25,000)	(35,000)	(20,000)
Closing		109,000	134,000	129,000

Asset schedule

A quick recap of our agenda is as follows:

- Record the historical profit and loss accounts and balance sheet
- Calculate the historical growth drivers
- Project the growth drivers for the profit and loss accounts and balance sheet

- Build up the projected profit and loss accounts and the balance sheet
- **Prepare the asset and depreciation schedule**
- Prepare the debt schedule
- Prepare the cash flow statement
- Ratio analysis
- DCF valuation
- Other valuations
- Scenario analysis

Our subject matter is referred to as long-term assets, fixed assets, and property plant and equipment. An asset is a long-term asset that the company will derive economic value from by using it for over a period of more than one year. This period is called the **useful life** of the asset. It would be unfair to charge the entire cost of such an asset in the period in which it was acquired; instead, the cost should be spread over the useful life of the asset.

This annual allocation of cost is a measure of the decrease in value of a fixed asset, through its use or the effluxion of time. This is called **depreciation**. It is usually expressed as a percentage and is charged to the profit and loss account for each year. The reduction in the value of the fixed asset is reflected in the balance sheet, where the total **accumulated depreciation** is deducted from the original cost and charged to date. This is referred to as the **net book value**.

The straight line method

If management decides that a useful service can be extracted from a fixed asset over a period of 10 years, then the cost of the asset will be spread over 10 years. The simplest way of doing this is to allocate the cost of the asset evenly over 10 years, in order to arrive at a fixed annual charge or depreciation rate of 10%. This is referred to as the **straight line method** (**SLM**) of depreciation.

Depreciation using SLM is calculated as follows:

$$\text{Depreciation} = \frac{\text{Cost of Asset}}{\text{Useful life}}$$

or

$$\text{Depreciation} = \text{Cost of Asset} \times \text{Depreciation rate}$$

The reducing balance method

Another method of calculating depreciation is called the **reducing balance method**. This method is based on the assumption that an asset loses value more quickly in earlier years. It is therefore constructed to allocate more depreciation in the early years and less in the later years of an asset's useful life. In the first year of depreciation, the depreciation rate is applied to the cost of the asset. In subsequent years, the depreciation rate is applied to the net book value brought forward from the previous year.

Since the net book value of the asset reduces from year to year, the depreciation will also reduce because the depreciation rate is being applied to a progressively lower figure. The following screenshot shows the difference between the straight line and reducing balance methods:

Depreciation Rate		10%	Useful Life	10years		
	Straight Line			**Reducing Balance**		
Year1	Cost	100,000,000		Cost		100,000,000
Year 1	Depreciation	10,000,000		Depreciation		10,000,000
Year2	Net book value	90,000,000		Net book value		90,000,000
Year2	Depreciation	10,000,000		Depreciation		9,000,000
Year 3	Net book value	80,000,000		Net book value		81,000,000
Year 3	Depreciation	10,000,000		Depreciation		8,100,000
Year 4	Net book value	70,000,000		Net book value		72,900,000
Year 4	Depreciation	10,000,000		Depreciation		7,290,000
Year5	Net book value	60,000,000		Net book value		65,610,000
Year5	Depreciation	10,000,000		Depreciation		6,561,000
Year 6	Net book value	50,000,000		Net book value		59,049,000
Year 6	Depreciation	10,000,000		Depreciation		5,904,900
Year 7	Net book value	40,000,000		Net book value		53,144,100
Year 7	Depreciation	10,000,000		Depreciation		5,314,410
Year 8	Net book value	30,000,000		Net book value		47,829,690
Year 8	Depreciation	10,000,000		Depreciation		4,782,969
Year 9	Net book value	20,000,000		Net book value		43,046,721
Year 9	Depreciation	10,000,000		Depreciation		4,304,672
Year 10	Net book value	10,000,000		Net book value		38,742,049
Year 10	Depreciation	10,000,000		Depreciation		3,874,205
	Net book value	-		Net book value		34,867,844

From the preceding screenshot, we can observe the following:

- Both methods begin with the same charge for depreciation—10,000,000 (100,000,000 x 10%)
- From the second year on, the depreciation for the year using the reducing balance method begins to drop from 10,000,000 to 9,000,000 in the second year, to 8,100,000 in the third year, and so on
- By the tenth year, the depreciation charge has dropped to 3,874,205
- With the SLM, the annual depreciation charge for the year remains constant at 10,000,000, up until the tenth year
- The net book value at the end of the tenth year with the SLM is zero, compared to 34,867,844 with the reducing balance method

The following is a graphical representation of the effect of the two depreciation methods on depreciation and net book value:

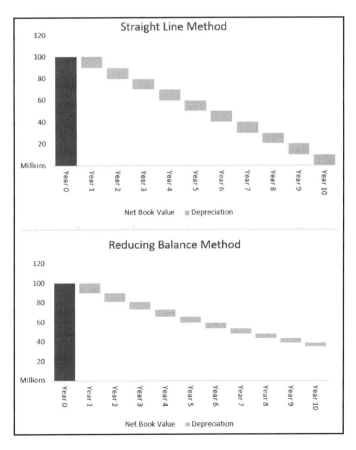

You should recognize that, no matter how old or utilized an asset becomes, it will always have a residual or scrap value. The residual value is an estimate of how much the asset would fetch if it were sold for scrap. With this in mind, you should ensure that you don't depreciate any assets down to zero, but rather down to their residual value, so that in the final year of depreciation, the depreciation charge will be the net book value minus the residual value. The following screenshot shows the annual depreciation for an asset with a `Residual value` of `1,000`:

Depreciation Rate		10%	Useful Life	10years
	Straight Line			
Year1	Cost	100,000,000		
Year 1	Depreciation	10,000,000		
Year2	Net book value	90,000,000		
Year2	Depreciation	10,000,000		
Year 3	Net book value	80,000,000		
Year 3	Depreciation	10,000,000		
Year 4	Net book value	70,000,000		
Year 4	Depreciation	10,000,000		
Year5	Net book value	60,000,000		
Year5	Depreciation	10,000,000		
Year 6	Net book value	50,000,000		
Year 6	Depreciation	10,000,000		
Year 7	Net book value	40,000,000		
Year 7	Depreciation	10,000,000		
Year 8	Net book value	30,000,000		
Year 8	Depreciation	10,000,000		
Year 9	Net book value	20,000,000		
Year 9	Depreciation	10,000,000		
Year 10	Net book value	10,000,000		Final year depreciation
Year 10	Depreciation	9,999,000		
	Residual value	1,000		Residual value

Apart from being more realistic, an asset with a residual value as net book value is less likely to disappear than one with a residual value of nil. Although the SLM and reducing balance method are the two most common methods of depreciation, there are other methods, such as sum-of-years digits and units of production.

Approaches to modeling assets

There are two approaches to modeling fixed assets, which are as follows:

- The detailed approach
- The simple approach

The detailed approach

The detailed approach is preferred and is a more precise method that looks at the components of fixed assets—the costs of the assets, additions, disposals, depreciation, and accumulated depreciation. Your discussions with management will give you an idea of their CapEx plans over the next five years. Where there is a disposal or sale, a fixed asset has to be removed from the books. The net book value (accumulated depreciation) of that asset will be transferred to a disposal account as a debit and the proceeds of the sale will be transferred to the same account as a credit. The difference between the two will either be a profit—where the **sale's proceeds** exceed the net book value—or a loss—where the net book value is greater than the sale's proceeds—on the disposal of assets and will be transferred from this disposal account to the profit and loss account at the end of the period. The following diagrams show the different scenarios associated with this.

The first diagram shows what happens when you profit on the disposal of assets:

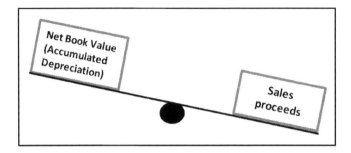

This means that you have sold the asset for an amount that is greater than its value according to the books.

The second diagram shows what happens when you make a loss on the disposal of assets:

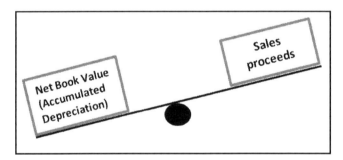

In this case, you have sold the asset for less than its value, as shown in the books, resulting in a loss on the disposal of assets. All of this is best captured in an asset and depreciation schedule, which should be prepared for each class of fixed assets and then consolidated into a general fixed asset schedule.

Asset and depreciation schedule

We will now prepare the schedule we talked about in the previous section, as follows:

				Yr1A	Yr2A	Yr3A	Yr4A	Yr5A	Yr6E
3	ASSET SCHEDULE			Yr1A	Yr2A	Yr3A	Yr4A	Yr5A	Yr6E
4		Depreciation Method	SLM						
5		Asset Life	Years	10	10	10	10	10	
6		Disposal of Assets	N Mn	-	-	-	-	-	
7									
8		Capex	N Mn	100,000	-	-	200,000	-	
9									
10		Depreciation Schedule							
11		Yr1A		10,000	10,000	10,000	10,000	10,000	
12		Yr2A			-	-	-	-	
13		Yr3A				-	-	-	
14		Yr4A					20,000	20,000	
15		Yr5A						-	
16		Yr6E							
17		Yr7E							
18		Yr8E							
19		Yr9E							
20		Yr10E							
21		Total Depreciation		10,000	10,000	10,000	30,000	30,000	
22									
23	Cost								
24		Opening Balance		-	100,000	100,000	100,000	300,000	
25		Add: Capex		100,000	-	-	200,000	-	
26		Less: Assets Sold/ Disposed		-	-	-	-	-	
27		Closing Balance		100,000	100,000	100,000	300,000	300,000	
28									
29		Accumulated Depreciation							
30		Opening Balance		-	10,000	20,000	30,000	60,000	
31		Add: Depreciation during current year		10,000	10,000	10,000	30,000	30,000	
32		Less: Depreciation on assets sold							
33		Closing Balance		10,000	20,000	30,000	60,000	90,000	
34									
35		Net Book Value		90,000	80,000	70,000	240,000	210,000	
36									
37									
38		Disposal Of Assets							
39		Cost of assets sold		-	-	-	-	-	
40		Depreciation on assets sold		-	-	-	-	-	
41		Net book value of assets sold		-	-	-	-	-	
42		Proceeds from sale of assets		-	-	-	-	-	
43									
44		(Profit)/loss on sale of assets							

This is the full asset and depreciation schedule that should be prepared for each asset class. We will now break the schedule down and analyze it in detail.

The first section contains the following information:

SCHEDULE		Yr1A	Yr2A	Yr3A	Yr4A	Yr5A	Yr6E
Depreciation Method	SLM						
Asset Life	Years	10	10	10	10	10	10
Disposal of Assets	N Mn	-	-	-	-	-	
Capex	N Mn	100,000	-	-	200,000	-	

Here, we have several keywords, such as `Depreciation Method` and `Asset Life`. We will look at what they are for this particular schedule:

- `Depreciation Method`: In our case, it is the `SLM`
- `Asset Life`: This is used to represent the useful life of the asset, which, in our case, is 10 years
- `Disposal of Assets`: This section is for the proceeds of the sale of fixed assets, if any are present
- `Capex`: This row shows how much was—and is projected to be—spent on fixed assets in each year

The next section is the `Depreciation Schedule`:

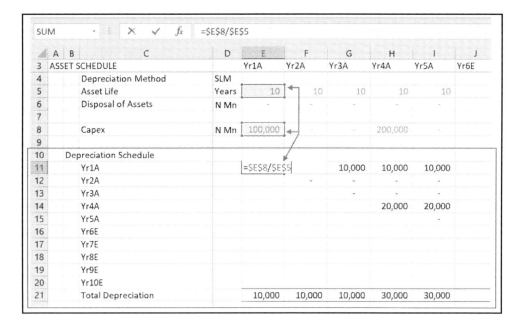

The depreciation on fixed assets is in rows **11-20** and across columns **E-N**. The annual depreciation charge on fixed asset additions is the CapEx of the year divided by the asset life. For Yr1A, this is **E8** divided by **E5**, which is 10,000, as shown in the preceding screenshot. The depreciation charge for Yr1A additions starts in **E11** and continues along row **11** at 10,000 each year for another 9 years, as shown in the following screenshot:

	A	B	C	D	E	F	G	H	I	J
3		ASSET SCHEDULE			Yr1A	Yr2A	Yr3A	Yr4A	Yr5A	Yr6E
4			Depreciation Method	SLM						
5			Asset Life	Years	10	10	10	10	10	
6			Disposal of Assets	N Mn	-	-	-	-	..	
7										
8			Capex	N Mn	100,000	-	-	200,000	-	
9										
10			Depreciation Schedule							
11			Yr1A		10,000	10,000	10,000	10,000	10,000	
12			Yr2A			-	-	-	-	
13			Yr3A				-	-	-	
14			Yr4A					20,000	20,000	
15			Yr5A						-	

Depreciation on additions in Yr2A is calculated as **F8** divided by **F5** and will be charged annually for 10 years along row **12**—the next row down—starting from **F12**. In the same way, depreciation on Yr3A additions will start from **G13** and will be charged for 10 years along row **13**.

The total depreciation charge for each year is the sum of all depreciation in rows **11-20** of the column for that year. For Yr1A, this will be the sum of all depreciation in rows **11–20** of column **E**; for Yr2A, this will be the sum of all depreciation in rows **11-20** of column **F**. In our example, only Yr1A and Yr4A have Capex additions during the year, as seen in the following screenshot:

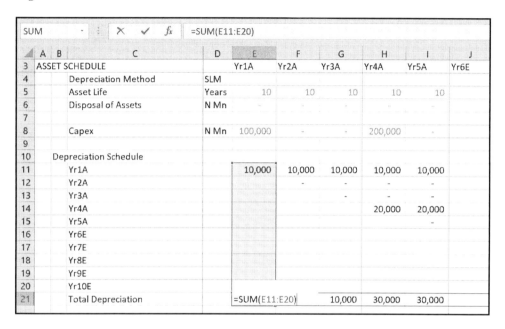

The next two sections are summaries of the cost and accumulated depreciation of the fixed assets, which are presented in the base and corkscrew layouts. The closing balance of costs for each year represents the total original or historical costs of fixed assets existing in the business at the end of each year. The following screenshot shows the Cost, Accumulated Depreciation, and Net Book Value:

SUM	▾	:	✕	✓	*fx*	=E27-E33				

A	B	C	D	E	F	G	H	I	J
3	ASSET SCHEDULE			Yr1A	Yr2A	Yr3A	Yr4A	Yr5A	Yr6E
22									
23	Cost								
24	Opening Balance			-	100,000	100,000	100,000	300,000	
25	Add: Capex			100,000	-	-	200,000	-	
26	Less: Assets Sold/ Disposed			-	-	-	-	-	
27	Closing Balance			100,000	100,000	100,000	300,000	300,000	
28									
29	Accumulated Depreciation								
30	Opening Balance			-	10,000	20,000	30,000	60,000	
31	Add: Depreciation during current year			10,000	10,000	10,000	30,000	30,000	
32	Less: Depreciation on assets sold								
33	Closing Balance			10,000	20,000	30,000	60,000	90,000	
34									
35	Net Book Value			=E27-E33	80,000	70,000	240,000	210,000	

Accumulated depreciation is the total amount of depreciation charged to date on fixed assets. Fixed assets are carried in the balance sheet at their net book value, which is cost less accumulated depreciation.

The simple approach

The simple approach to projecting fixed assets is to model them using a fixed assets turnover ratio, as illustrated in the following formula:

$$\text{Fixed asset turnover} = \frac{\text{Turnover...}}{\text{Fixed assets}}$$

As in our previous examples, we start with historical data and calculate the fixed asset and turnover ratio for each of the historical years. The following screenshot shows the calculation of the `Fixed asset turnover ratio` field:

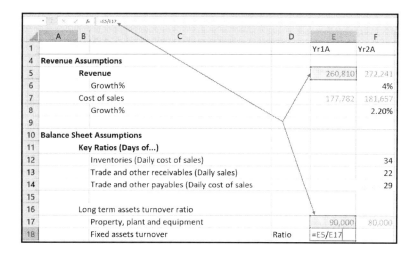

We would calculate the average of the historical fixed assets turnover ratios over `Yr1A`-`Yr5A`, and then use this average as the projected driver for the next five years. The following screenshot illustrates the calculation of the average of the historical fixed asset turnover ratios:

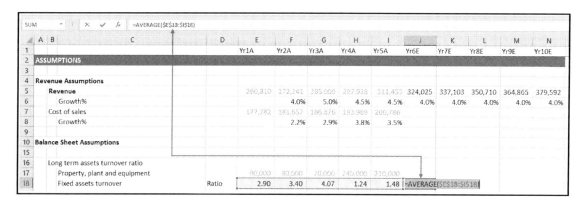

Depreciation can be derived as follows:

1. Divide the historical cost of fixed assets for each year by the depreciation charge for their respective year, in order to arrive at the average useful life of assets for that year:

		f_x	=E56/E57			
A	B	C		D	E	F
1					Yr1A	Yr2A
54						
55						
56	Cost				90,000	80
57	Depreciation				10,000	20
58	Useful life				=E56/E57	
59						

2. You then calculate the average for the useful life values of the past five historical years:

		f_x	=AVERAGE($E$58:$I$58)								
A	B	C	D	E	F	G	H	I	J	K
1				Yr1A	Yr2A	Yr3A	Yr4A	Yr5A	Yr6E	Yr7E
54										
55										
56	Cost			90,000	80,000	70,000	240,000	210,000	123,702	128,695
57	Depreciation			10,000	20,000	30,000	60,000	90,000		
58	Useful life			9.0	4.0	2.3	4.0	2.3	=AVERAGE($E$58:$I$58)	
59										

3. Now, enter the Useful life value into the following equation in order to arrive at the Depreciation charge for the year:

$$\text{Depreciation} = \frac{\text{Cost of Asset}}{\text{Useful life}}$$

The preceding step will result in the following value:

		f_x	=J56/J58							
A	B	C	D	E	F	G	H	I	J	
1				Yr1A	Yr2A	Yr3A	Yr4A	Yr5A	Yr6E	Yr7E
54										
55										
56	Cost			90,000	80,000	70,000	240,000	210,000	123,702	128
57	Depreciation			10,000	20,000	30,000	60,000	90,000	=J56/J58	
58	Useful life			9.0	4.0	2.3	4.0	2.3	4.3	
59										

4. Now, extend the formula for each of the projected years:

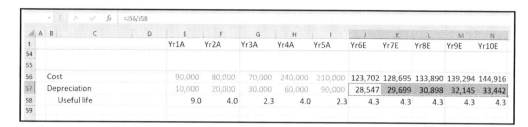

			Yr1A	Yr2A	Yr3A	Yr4A	Yr5A	Yr6E	Yr7E	Yr8E	Yr9E	Yr10E
56	Cost		90,000	80,000	70,000	240,000	210,000	123,702	128,695	133,890	139,294	144,916
57	Depreciation		10,000	20,000	30,000	60,000	90,000	28,547	29,699	30,898	32,145	33,442
58	Useful life		9.0	4.0	2.3	4.0	2.3	4.3	4.3	4.3	4.3	4.3

Debt schedule

A company's capital is made up of debt and equity, and most businesses try to maintain a steady ratio between debt and equity (a leverage ratio). The debt schedule is part of our forecast of capital structure.

The following list shows our current agenda:

- Record the historical profit and loss accounts and balance sheet
- Calculate the historical growth drivers
- Project the growth drivers for the profit and loss accounts and balance sheet
- Build up the projected profit and loss accounts and balance sheet
- Prepare the asset and depreciation schedule
- **Prepare the debt schedule**
- Prepare the cash flow statement
- Ratio analysis
- DCF valuation
- Other valuations
- Scenario analysis

As with fixed assets, forecasting debt can be done in one of two ways; a detailed complex method or a quick and simple method.

In addition, we need to consider the treatment of interest. The question is, do we take interest on the opening or closing balance of debt or do we apply the interest rate to the average debt for the year?

The complex approach

If your model requires a high level of precision, you will start by getting as much information as possible from published historical accounts and management discussions. You would look out for plans to obtain additional finance and liquidate existing loans, and additions to fixed assets that will require finance.

In addition, companies often publish information about maturing loans. You would use this to project annual repayments and ensure that these repayments are stopped once the respective loan has been paid off. The following screenshot presents a debt schedule:

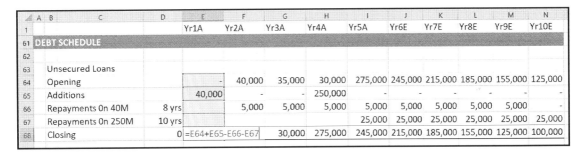

				Yr1A	Yr2A	Yr3A	Yr4A	Yr5A	Yr6E	Yr7E	Yr8E	Yr9E	Yr10E
61	**DEBT SCHEDULE**												
62													
63	Unsecured Loans												
64	Opening			-	40,000	35,000	30,000	275,000	245,000	215,000	185,000	155,000	125,000
65	Additions			40,000	-	-	250,000	-	-	-	-	-	-
66	Repayments On 40M	8 yrs			5,000	5,000	5,000	5,000	5,000	5,000	5,000	5,000	-
67	Repayments On 250M	10 yrs						25,000	25,000	25,000	25,000	25,000	25,000
68	Closing		0	=E64+E65-E66-E67		30,000	275,000	245,000	215,000	185,000	155,000	125,000	100,000

We prepare a debt schedule using the base and corkscrew layouts.

In our example, there was a N40 million loan taken out in Yr1A, at 10% interest, repayable over 8 years; and a N250 million loan taken out in Yr4A, also at 10% interest, repayable over 10 years. The N40 million loan is repaid over 8 years, from Yr2A to Yr9E. Repayment of the N250 million loan does not start until Yr5A and will continue for another 9 years.

In this complex model, you will calculate interest on the average loan outstanding. The average loan outstanding is the opening outstanding plus closing debts divided by two. The following screenshot is an illustration of a debt schedule with the interest calculated on the average debt outstanding:

	A B	C	D	E	F	G	H	I	J	K	L	M	N
1				Yr1A	Yr2A	Yr3A	Yr4A	Yr5A	Yr6E	Yr7E	Yr8E	Yr9E	Yr10E
61	DEBT SCHEDULE												
62													
63		Unsecured Loans											
64		Opening		-	40,000	35,000	30,000	275,000	245,000	215,000	185,000	155,000	125,000
65		Additions		40,000	-	-	250,000	-	-	-	-	-	-
66		Repayments On 40M	8 yrs		5,000	5,000	5,000	5,000	5,000	5,000	5,000	5,000	-
67		Repayments On 250M	10 yrs					25,000	25,000	25,000	25,000	25,000	25,000
68		Closing	0	40,000	35,000	30,000	275,000	245,000	215,000	185,000	155,000	125,000	100,000
69													
70		Interest rate		10%	10%	10%	10%	10%	10%	10%	10%	10%	10%
71		Interest		=AVERAGE(E64,E68)*E70			15,250	26,000	23,000	20,000	17,000	14,000	11,250

The interest is calculated as follows:

$$\text{Interest} = \frac{(\text{opening debt} + \textbf{closing debt})}{2} \times \text{interest rate}$$

The closing debt is calculated as follows:

$$\textbf{Closing debt} = \text{opening debt} + \text{interest}$$

For ease of understanding, let's assume that there's no repayment. The closing debt will be the opening debt plus accrued interest. The following screenshot shows the debt schedule with a closing balance, including accrued interest:

16	Unsecured Loans											
17	Opening		-	40,000	35,000	30,000	275,000	270,000	265,000	260,000	255,000	250,000
18	Additions		40,000	-	-	250,000	-	-	-	-	-	-
19	Repayments On 40M	8 yrs		5,000	5,000	5,000	5,000	5,000	5,000	5,000	5,000	5,000
20	Repayments On 250M	10 yrs										
21	Interest											
22												
23	Closing	0	=E17+E18-E19-E20+E21			275,000	270,000	265,000	260,000	255,000	250,000	245,000
24												
25	Interest rate		10%	10%	10%	10%	10%	10%	10%	10%	10%	10%
26												

Cover | Financial Model | scenarios | Sheet1 | comps | ⊕

Edit

The following screenshot shows the formula to calculate interest by including both opening and closing debt balances:

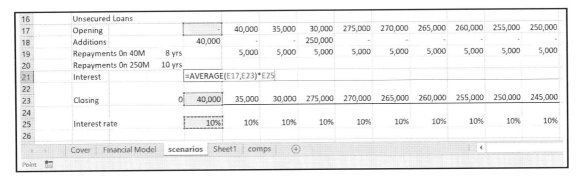

In the previous two screenshots, we can see how the formula to calculate the closing balance includes interest and the formula to calculate interest includes the closing debt balance. This creates a circular reference, which is flagged as an error by Excel.

The following screenshot shows how Excel flags a circular reference:

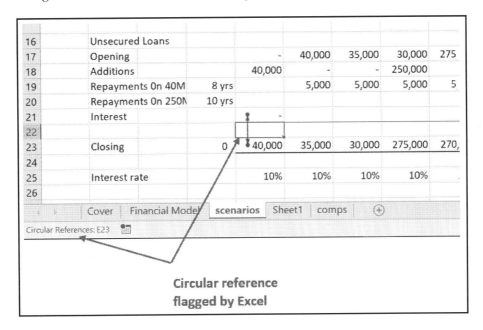

In order to stop the iterations or the continuous calculation of such a formula, Excel flags the formula as a circular reference. Sometimes, you create a circular reference on purpose to achieve a desired result. In our case, we wish to use the most accurate method at our disposal to forecast the interest—utilizing average interest instead of opening or closing debt.

Closing debt is used to calculate interest, which is then used to calculate closing debt. This represents one iteration. This latter closing debt will result in a value that is slightly different from the original closing debt used in the calculation of interest. After the second iteration, the difference is reduced, and it continues to reduce with each successive iteration until it becomes negligible and the two values for closing debt are effectively equal.

In order to allow this to happen without Excel picking it up as an error, you will need to enable iterative calculations under **Excel Options**>**Formulas**. The following screenshot demonstrates how to enable iterations:

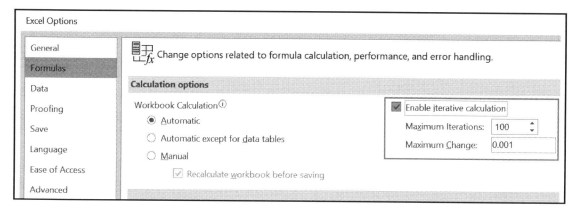

In Excel 2016, click **File**>**Options**. This will launch the Excel options dialog box. Then, click on **Formulas** and check the **Enable iterative calculation** box. Accept the default **Maximum Iterations** of **100**. This means that Excel believes that after 100 iterations, the difference generated by each iteration becomes negligible or immaterial.

 You should always remember to go back and uncheck the **Enable iterative calculation** box. Otherwise, an unintended circular reference may go undetected and could cause Excel to crash, resulting in a loss of information.

The simple approach

If that level of precision is not required, you could adopt a simpler approach, using the leverage ratio:

$$\text{leverage ratio} = \frac{\text{Debt}}{\text{Equity}}$$

Generally, companies do not frequently change their share capital. It is therefore reasonable to assume that the share capital will remain the same, and that equity will only be affected by retained earnings. Thus, leverage ratio multiplied by equity will give us our debt. For interest, you simply apply the interest rate to the opening debt balance. This will avoid any circular references.

An even simpler method is to consider that, as companies repay old debts, they generally take on new debts. You could therefore assume that the debt balance stays the same. You will forecast the interest charge for the year by applying the interest rate to the opening balance of long-term debt.

Once we have updated our balance sheet and profit and loss accounts with our calculations, the only outstanding item that is needed to complete the 3-statement model will be cash.

Now that we have learned everything about historical data, let's apply it to create a loan amortization schedule, as seen in the next section.

Creating a loan amortization schedule

Let's assume that you work at a bank and a customer has requested a home loan. However, the customer doesn't want any of the pre-made packages on offer and wants a customized loan for a specific tenure and amount. In such cases, the calculations to compute the detailed schedule might take a lot of time, which is valuable when it comes to dealing with customers. It would be really useful to have a unique model tailored to your needs, which can easily compute values for all kinds of loans. We will now learn how to create one such schedule here, implementing most of the things we have learned in this chapter.

Creating the template

Our first step is to create a common template that can be used for all purposes. We will do this by taking the following steps:

1. The first thing to do is create a template for calculating the loan. We will do this by first creating a two-by-four table for entering the variables in the loan, as follows:

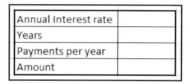

2. We will now add data validation to the **Payments per year** field, so that we can choose between four options of payment—semi-monthly, monthly, quarterly, and yearly. For this, we will first create a table containing 4 values—24, 12, 4, and 1, as seen here:

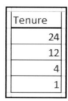

3. Now, we need to convert this table into a list. We will do that by going to the **Formulas** tab and selecting the **Define Name** option, as shown here:

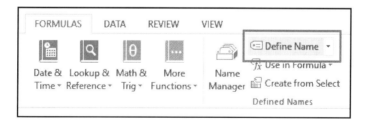

4. In the pop-up window that follows, we will define the name of the list, which I have entered as `Tenure`. In the **Refers to:** input box, we will enter the cell array where the table is present, which in this case is `$J$2:$J$5`:

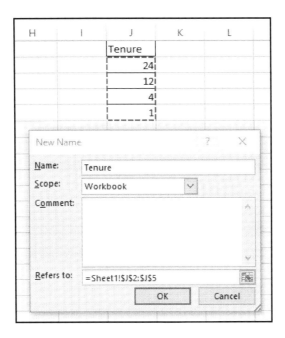

5. Once everything has been entered, go ahead and click on **OK**. Our list has now been defined.

6. Our next step is to add this list in the `Payments per year` field. For this, navigate to the **Data** tab, and select the **Data Validation** option there:

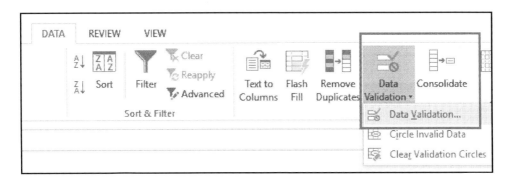

7. In the pop-up window that appears, open the **Allow:** drop-down menu and select **List**, as shown here:

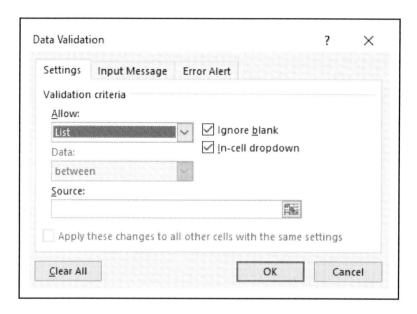

8. Now, in the **Source:** input field, press *F3* on your keyboard to open the **Paste Name** popup. This is where you will find the name of your list, as seen here:

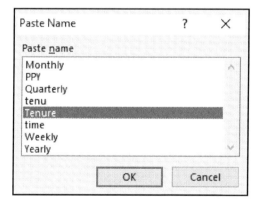

9. Click on **OK** after selecting the name of your list and it should appear in the **Source:** input field. Now, click on **OK** in the **Data Validation** window, and lo and behold, the dropdown has been created in the `Payments per year` field, as shown in the following screenshot:

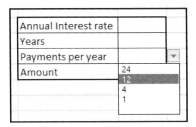

10. Our final step is to create the actual loan schedule table, which should look similar to the one in the following screenshot:

Payment Number	Payment	Principal	Interest	Balance
1				

Thus, we have now created a template where we can implement our loan schedule, as shown in the following screenshot:

					Tenure
Annual Interest rate					24
Years					12
Payments per year					4
Amount					1

Payment Number	Payment	Principal	Interest	Balance	
1					

Now comes the hard part—creating the formulas required to calculate each of the elements in the loan schedule.

Creating the formulas

Now that we have our template all ready to go, it's time to work our magic with Excel and create formulas for calculating the different variables that are part of a loan, such as the principal amount, the interest amount, the total payment to be made, and the balance amount after payment. If we try to enter the actual formulas that we used to calculate each value, the formulas will become way too complicated for us. Thankfully, Excel has made it easy for us to calculate such values with the help of built-in functions such as PMT, PPMT, and IPMT. We will use these functions here to calculate our loan, using the following steps:

1. Picking up where we left off after creating the template, we will start entering the formulas we need into the loan schedule table we created previously. Our first formula utilizes the PMT function, which can be used to easily calculate the total amount to be paid for a specific period. The PMT formula takes the following arguments:

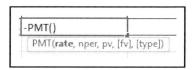

   Here, rate is the rate of interest per period, which is calculated by dividing the annual rate of interest by the number of years the loan is active. The nper variable is the total number of payments in the duration of the loan, which is calculated by multiplying the number of years and the number of payments per year. The pv variable is the principal amount of the loan. The fv and type variables are optional, and we won't be using them here.

2. In our case, the PMT formula should be as follows:

   ```
   =PMT(Annual Interest rate/Payments per year, Years*Payments per
   year, Amount)
   ```

   We will replace those variables with the actual values—with the help of cell referencing—so that our final formula is as follows:

   ```
   =PMT($C$2/$C$4,$C$3*$C$4,$C$5)
   ```

3. Now that the first formula is in place, we will calculate the principal amount using the PPMT function, which takes the following arguments:

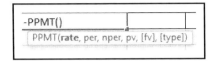

This formula is similar to the PMT formula we saw previously; the only difference is that we are accounting for the current payment number, which is the per variable. Thus, our formula for the principal amount will be as follows:

```
=PPMT($C$2/$C$4,$A8,$C$3*$C$4,$C$5)
```

4. The next formula we need to add is the one to calculate the interest amount. We will use the IPMT function to do this, which takes the following arguments:

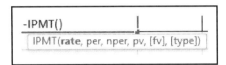

This formula is an exact replica of the PPMT formula, except that we are using the IPMT function instead of PPMT:

```
=IPMT($C$2/$C$4,$A8,$C$3*$C$4,$C$5)
```

5. The last formula that we need to enter is the one that calculates the balance amount after each payment. This one is pretty simple cell referencing, since we just need to deduct the principal amount from the previous balance amount. For the first payment, the previous balance amount will be the total loan amount, as shown here:

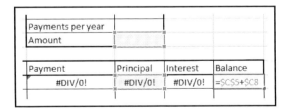

Now that we have prepared all the formulas for the schedule, let's start calculating loans!

Using the schedule

Assume that a customer has approached you and requested a loan of $10,000 for a duration of 2 years. As per the company policy, you have to charge them an annual interest rate of 5%. Also, the customer wants to opt for monthly payments. Let's calculate the loan for them, using the following steps:

1. We will input all the variables that the customer has requested, as seen in the following screenshot:

Annual Interest rate	5.00%
Years	2
Payments per year	12
Amount	10,000

2. We can see that the values for the first payment have been calculated:

Payment Number	Payment	Principal	Interest	Balance
1	($438.71)	($397.05)	($41.67)	$9,602.95

 Red values indicate deductions, which will be subtracted from the original amounts.

3. Now, we will select the **A8 – E8** range and drag the fill handle down one row, in order to populate the second column. This results in the following output:

Payment Number	Payment	Principal	Interest	Balance
1	($438.71)	($397.05)	($41.67)	$9,602.95
2	($438.71)	($398.70)	($40.01)	$9,601.30

Here, we will notice that the payment, principal, and interest rates have been updated normally, but the balance has decreased by only $1. That can't be right, can it? This happens because, as we mentioned in the previous section, we need to deduct the principal amount from the previous balance amount, which in the first column, was the total loan amount. From the second installment onward, the balance has to be calculated from the previous period's balance amount.

4. We need to modify the formula in the **Balance** column, so that the first cell referenced is E8, where the initial balance amount is present. Ensure that you don't lock the column while doing so. Our formula for the second balance field is now the following:

    ```
    =$E8+$C9
    ```

   This leads to the correct output, as shown here:

		f_x	=$E8+$C9	
A	B	C	D	E
	Annual Interest rate	5.00%		
	Years	2		
	Payments per year	12		
	Amount	10,000		
Number	Payment	Principal	Interest	Balance
1	($438.71)	($397.05)	($41.67)	$9,602.95
2	($438.71)	($398.70)	($40.01)	$9,204.25

5. Now, we can simply select the second range, which is **A9 – E9**, and drag the fill handle down 22 rows so that we can see all the payment periods, as shown in the following screenshot:

Payment Number	Payment	Principal	Interest	Balance
1	($438.71)	($397.05)	($41.67)	$9,602.95
2	($438.71)	($398.70)	($40.01)	$9,204.25
3	($438.71)	($400.36)	($38.35)	$8,803.89
4	($438.71)	($402.03)	($36.68)	$8,401.86
5	($438.71)	($403.71)	($35.01)	$7,998.15
6	($438.71)	($405.39)	($33.33)	$7,592.76
7	($438.71)	($407.08)	($31.64)	$7,185.69
8	($438.71)	($408.77)	($29.94)	$6,776.91
9	($438.71)	($410.48)	($28.24)	$6,366.44
10	($438.71)	($412.19)	($26.53)	$5,954.25
11	($438.71)	($413.90)	($24.81)	$5,540.34
12	($438.71)	($415.63)	($23.08)	$5,124.71
13	($438.71)	($417.36)	($21.35)	$4,707.35
14	($438.71)	($419.10)	($19.61)	$4,288.25
15	($438.71)	($420.85)	($17.87)	$3,867.41
16	($438.71)	($422.60)	($16.11)	$3,444.81
17	($438.71)	($424.36)	($14.35)	$3,020.45
18	($438.71)	($426.13)	($12.59)	$2,594.32
19	($438.71)	($427.90)	($10.81)	$2,166.41
20	($438.71)	($429.69)	($9.03)	$1,736.73
21	($438.71)	($431.48)	($7.24)	$1,305.25
22	($438.71)	($433.28)	($5.44)	$871.97
23	($438.71)	($435.08)	($3.63)	$436.89
24	($438.71)	($436.89)	($1.82)	($0.00)

We can see that the last balance amount shown is $0.00. This means that our loan has been paid off completely!

Thus, we have created a loan amortization schedule in Excel. You can now play around with it, and maybe use it to calculate your own loans, or any loans that you may be planning to take in the near future!

Summary

In this chapter, we have seen the importance of fixed asset and debt schedules. We have illustrated how they affect balance sheets, profit and loss accounts, and cash flow statements. We have learned about the base and corkscrew methods, as well as complex and simple approaches to preparing fixed assets, depreciation, and debt schedules.

In the next chapter, we will perform our final calculations and prepare the cash flows in order to arrive at the accurate statement, which should cause our balance sheets to balance and conclude the 3-statement model.

7
Cash Flow Statement

The following list shows our agenda and the next stage is the preparation of the cash flow statement:

- Record the historical profit and loss and balance sheet
- Calculate the historical growth drivers
- Project the growth drivers for the profit and loss accounts and balance sheet
- Build up the projected profit and loss accounts and balance sheet
- Prepare the asset and depreciation schedule
- Prepare the debt schedule
- **Prepare the cash flow statement**
- Ratio analysis
- DCF valuation
- Other valuations
- Scenario analysis

At this stage, we have completed the profit and loss account and the only item left to complete the balance sheet, which is still out of balance, is cash. In this chapter, we will look at how to prepare the cash flow statement for our project.

In this chapter, we will cover the following topics:

- Introduction to the cash flow statement
- Items not involving the movement of cash
- Net change in working capital
- Balancing the balance sheet
- Creating a quick cash flow statement

Introduction to the cash flow statement

Profit and loss accounts are different from the cash flow statement in that they do not wait for the cash implications of a transaction to be settled before the transaction is recognized. For example, if you make a sale of N100,000 and the customer has received the goods or services but has not yet paid, there is no cash movement.

However, both you and the customer recognize that a sale has been made—indeed, ownership and custody of the goods have been transferred, so the profit and loss account will record this as a credit sale, increasing turnover by N100,000, and to complete the double entry, a receivable is created under that customer's name to signify that they owe you N100,000. This is the accrual basis of accounting, which says that income should be recorded in the period in which it is earned, and expenses should be matched with the income they have helped generate.

This permeates throughout accounts, affecting things such as rent paid in advance (only the rent for this year should go through the profit and loss accounts); electricity used but the bill has not yet arrived (charge the electricity in the profit and loss accounts); and purchases must be adjusted by opening and closing stock so that only the cost of goods sold is reflected in the profit and loss account.

In all of these examples, the actual cash flow will differ from the amount included in the profit and loss account. This makes good economic sense and is essential in order to arrive at the true profit or loss for each period. However, as quoted earlier, turnover is vanity, profit is sanity, but cash is reality. No matter how much profit a company is making, if it is not backed up by cash, sooner or later the company will go bust. This is why the cash flow statement is so important.

You will recall that we created a visual check in our model to indicate whether the balance sheets are in or out of balance. So, if they are out of balance, the check cells will be red but the moment they fall in balance the cells will turn to green, as shown in the following screenshots. The historical balance sheets will of course be in balance. The following screenshot illustrates the position with the forecast years out of balance:

	YO1A	YO2A	YO3A	YO4F	YO5F	YO6F	YO7F	YO8F
Balance Check	TRUE	TRUE	TRUE	FALSE	FALSE	FALSE	FALSE	FALSE
(Unless otherwise specified, all financials an Units								
CASH FLOW STATEMENT								
Cashflow from Operating Activities								
PAT		13,787	1,850	13,309	13,318	23,312	33,684	44,449
Add: Depreciation		10,000	10,000	30,000	30,000	30,000	30,000	30,000
Add: Interest Expense		3,750	3,250	15,250	26,000	23,000	20,000	17,000
Net Change in Working Capital								
Add: Increase in Accounts payable		3,524	(223)	(1,759)	1,865	(1,758)	1,866	(1,758)
Less: Increase in Inventory		(2,462)	(3,724)	7,201	(7,331)	7,201	(7,331)	7,201
Less: Increase in Account Receivables		(10,704)	(4,333)	2,089	(5,252)	1,946	(5,402)	1,789
Net Change in Working Capital		(9,642)	(8,280)	7,532	(10,717)	7,389	(10,867)	7,232
Cashflow from Operations		17,895	6,820	66,091	58,600	83,701	72,816	98,681

In assembling financial statements, the cash flow statement is usually prepared from the balance sheet and profit and loss account. The net inflow or outflow of cash is then added to or subtracted from the opening balance of cash to arrive at the closing balance of cash and cash equivalents, which should agree with the corresponding figure on the balance sheet. For the forecast years, there is no cash figure on the balance sheet, so we need to take advantage of this balance sheet-cash flow relationship to project a figure for cash.

Prepare the cash flow statement as usual, ending with a figure for the closing cash balance. Then, we post this figure to the balance sheet as cash and cash equivalents. If the balance sheet now balances, this indicates that our model up to this stage is mathematically correct. Otherwise, we will begin the tedious process of troubleshooting to trace the error:

		Y01A	Y02A	Y03A	Y04F	Y05F	Y06F	Y07F	Y08F
4	Balance Check	TRUE	TRUE	TRUE	TRUE	TRUE	TRUE	TRUE	TRUE
6	(Unless otherwise specified, all financials an Units								
113	CASH FLOW STATEMENT								
115	**Cashflow from Operating Activities**								
116	PAT	13,787	1,850	13,309	13,318	23,312	33,684	44,449
117	Add: Depreciation	10,000	10,000	30,000	30,000	30,000	30,000	30,000
118	Add: Interest Expense	3,750	3,250	15,250	26,000	23,000	20,000	17,000
120	**Net Change in Working Capital**								
121	Add: Increase in Accounts payable	3,524	(223)	(1,759)	1,865	(1,758)	1,866	(1,758)
122	Less: Increase in Inventory	(2,462)	(3,724)	7,201	(7,331)	7,201	(7,331)	7,201
123	Less: Increase in Account Receivables	(10,704)	(4,333)	2,089	(5,252)	1,946	(5,402)	1,789
124	**Net Change in Working Capital**	(9,642)	(8,280)	7,532	(10,717)	7,389	(10,867)	7,232
126	**Cashflow from Operations**	17,895	6,820	66,091	58,600	83,701	72,816	98,681
128	**Cashflow from Investment Activities**								
129	Less: Capex	-	-	(200,000)	-	-	-	-
130	Add: Proceeds from Disposal of Assets								
131	Less: Increase in WIP								
132	Less: Increase in Investments	648	(6,557)	(40,000)	-	-	-	-
133	**Cashflow from Investment Activities**	648	(6,557)	(240,000)	-	-	-	-
135	**Cashflow from Financing Activities**								
136	Add: New Equity Raised								
137	Add: New Unsecured Loans Raised	-	-	250,000	-	-	-	-
138	Less: Unsecured Loans Repaid	(5,000)	(5,000)	(5,000)	(30,000)	(30,000)	(30,000)	(30,000)
139	Less: Dividends Paid								
140	Less: Interest Expense	(3,750)	(3,250)	(15,250)	(26,000)	(23,000)	(20,000)	(17,000)
141	**Cashflow from Financing Activities**	(8,750)	(8,250)	229,750	(56,000)	(53,000)	(50,000)	(47,000)
143	**Net Cashflow**	9,793	(7,987)	55,841	2,600	30,701	22,816	51,681
145	**Cash Balance**								
146	Opening Balance	7,459	17,252	9,265	65,106	67,707	98,408	121,224
147	Net Cashflow	9,793	(7,987)	55,841	2,600	30,701	22,816	51,681
148	**Closing Balance**	17,252	9,265	65,106	67,707	98,408	121,224	172,905

The preceding screenshot shows the completed cash flow statement, wherein the closing cash balances have now been posted to the appropriate balance sheets and the balance check shows that they are all now in balance. The logical starting point in the preparation of the cash flow statement is the profit for the year.

Items not involving the movement of cash

In arriving at PAT, a number of items not involving the movement of cash have been considered, which now have to be reversed in order to arrive at an accurate figure for cash flow, as shown here:

6	(Unless otherwise specified, all financials a Units	Y01A	Y02A	Y03A
113	**CASH FLOW STATEMENT**			
114				
115	**Cashflow from Operating Activities**			
116	PAT		13,787	1,850
117	Add: Depreciation		10,000	10,000
118	Add: Interest Expense		3,750	3,250
119				

The obvious candidate for this is depreciation. The relevant cash flow occurs at the time the asset is purchased. However, we don't charge the total cost to the profit and loss account all at once; the correct accounting treatment is to allocate the original cost over the useful life of the asset.

This periodic allocation of cost is called **depreciation** and clearly does not involve the movement of cash. Since it has been deducted as an expense in arriving at our profit, we need to add it back to the PAT, as shown in the preceding screenshot. We also add back interest charged to PAT. Although this is cash flow, it is the cost of debt finance, and hence, is more appropriately treated under financing activities.

Net change in working capital

Let's look at the following screenshot on the net change in working capital:

6	(Unless otherwise specified, all financials a Units	Y01A	Y02A	Y03A	Y04F
119					
120	**Net Change in Working Capital**				
121	Add: Increase in Accounts payable			3,524	(223)
122	Less: Increase in Inventory			(2,462)	(3,724)
123	Less: Increase in Account Receivables			(10,704)	(4,333)
124	**Net Change in Working Capital**			(9,642)	(8,280)

This section converts our profit from the accrual basis into cash-based profit. In simple terms, taking our previous example, we have recorded a sale of N100,000, increasing our profit by that amount even though no cash was received. This section looks at the corresponding increase in accounts receivable of N100,000 and treats it as an outflow to be deducted before arriving at cash flow from operating activities, hence reversing the inflow recorded from the credit sale.

In summary, under this section, we add increases in working capital liabilities and subtract increases in working capital assets. An increase is manifested when we subtract the current year's figure from the previous year's, assuming that this year's figure is higher than that of the previous year.

 Note that if you stick to this language, decreases will automatically take care of themselves.

Let's look at the following table:

	YR2	YR1
1. Accounts Payable	50,000	30,000
2. Accounts Payable	50,000	70,000

If you consider the increase to be (**YR2 - YR1**), then in example 1, `Add: Increase in Accounts payable` will give the following:

$$+ (50,000 - 30,000) = 20,000 \text{ an inflow}$$

In example 2, where there is a decrease, we will get the following:

$$+ (50,000 - 70,000) = +(-20,000) = -20,000 \text{ an outflow}$$

The same goes for working capital assets, as seen in the following table:

	YR2	YR1
1. Accounts Receivable	40,000	35,000
2. Accounts Receivable	50,000	60,000

As in the preceding, the increase is (**YR2 - YR1**), so in example 1, `Less: Increase in Accounts Receivable` will give the following:

$$- (40,000 - 35,000) = - 5,000 \text{ an outflow}$$

In example 2, where there is a decrease, we will get the following:

$$- (50,000 - 60,000) = -(-10,000) = +10,000 \text{ an inflow}$$

The subtotal of everything so far gives us cash flow from operating activities.

Cash flow from investment activities

Let's look at the following screenshot on cash flow from investment activities:

6	(Unless otherwise specified, all financials a Units	Y01A	Y02A	Y03A	Y04F
128	**Cashflow from Investment Activities**				
129	Less: Capex			-	-
130	Add: Proceeds from Disposal of Assets				
131	Less: Increase in WIP				
132	Less: Increase in Investments			648	(6,557)
133	**Cashflow from Investment Activities**			**648**	**(6,557)**

This section is fairly self-explanatory. It involves the purchase or sale of investments, including shares in other companies, CapEx, and so on.

Cash flow from financing activities

Let's look at the following screenshot on cash flow from financing activities:

6	(Unless otherwise specified, all financials a Units	Y01A	Y02A	Y03A	Y04F
134					
135	**Cashflow from Financing Activities**				
136	Add: New Equity Raised				
137	Add: New Unsecured Loans Raised			-	-
138	Less: Unsecured Loans Repaid			(5,000)	(5,000)
139	Less: Dividends Paid				
140	Less: Interest Expense			(3,750)	(3,250)
141	**Cashflow from Financing Activities**			**(8,750)**	**(8,250)**

By now, we should be comfortable with the fact that financing comes from internal sources, equity (shares), or external sources in the form of debt. Increases and decreases in these balances are treated here. You will recall that we added back interest charges to the PAT. That was in order to deal with it here, under financing activities. We will also deduct dividends paid as an outflow.

Under financing and investing activities, there will occasionally be large, one-off transactions that have a significant effect on the net cash flow; for example, the sale of fixed assets. Operational activities, however, reflect the ordinary business activities of the company. This is where investors look to determine whether a company generates enough cash to settle its liabilities and for growth.

Balancing the balance sheet

The closing cash balance will be posted to the balance sheet as cash and cash equivalent under current assets. However, it is important to note that the balance could be negative, in which case, it should be reflected as an overdraft under current liabilities. Since you don't know which it is going to be, especially as it may change as a result of subsequent modifications, you need to build your model in such a way that the cash balance is posted to cash and cash equivalents if it is positive and to overdraft if it is negative.

Usually, when you need to model a situation that depends on a logical question (one that results in a true or false answer), the first thing that springs to mind is the IF statement. For example, say the cursor is in cell **J35**, cash and cash equivalents, and you wish to relate this to the calculated cash balance from the cash flow statement in cell **J86**.

You would type =J86, and the cash balance would appear in cell **J35** when you press *Enter*.

To incorporate the uncertainty explained in the preceding section with the IF statement, you would type =IF(J86>0,J86,""). This states that if the cash balance is positive, greater than 0, then put the cash balance in cell **J35**; otherwise, leave the cell blank.

In the corresponding overdraft cell, say cell **J45**, you would type =IF(J86>0,"",-J86). This states that if the cash balance is positive, greater than 0, then leave the cell blank; otherwise, change the cash balance sign from negative to positive and put it in cell **J45**.

However, there is a more elegant way to handle this using the MIN and MAX formulas.

In cell **J35**, you would simply type = MAX(J86,0). This formula will ensure that the maximum of the cash balance and 0 always goes in cell **J35**.

If you think about it, a positive number is always greater than 0 and will therefore always be treated as cash and cash equivalents. In cell **J45**, Overdraft, you would type =MIN(J86,0).

This will ensure that whenever the cash balance is negative, it will always be posted in cell **J45**; otherwise the cell will be 0. Once this posting has been done, the balance sheets should balance and our balance check cells should all have turned green. If this is not the case, then you will need to troubleshoot to locate the source of the error.

Troubleshooting

The first step is to check the accuracy of your cash flow statement. Since the historical years will already have a cash or overdraft balance, you can check your cash flow cash balances for those years against the cash on the balance sheet.

If they do not agree, you will need to check your cash flow entries again:

1. First of all, check your totals for any casting errors.
2. Next, determine what the difference is and divide by 2. Look through your cash flow to see if there is an amount equal to this figure. This test checks to see whether you have wrongly posted a figure as negative instead of positive or vice versa.
3. Scan through the balance sheet and profit and loss account for an amount equal to the whole difference calculated in step 1. This test checks to see whether you have omitted an amount from the cash flow.
4. Scan through the balance sheet and profit and loss to see whether there are any accounts or balances that have not been accounted for in your cash flow. This often happens where you have irregular accounts or movements; for example, share premiums, special reserves, and prior year adjustments.
5. Once you have reconciled your historical cash flow statements to the historical balance sheets, your balance checks should now be all green. If they are not, then you will need to widen your troubleshooting to the rest of the model.

Circular references

Say you have data in cells **A1** to **A4** and you type the following formula in cell **A5**—=SUM(A1:A6). This will be flagged by Excel as a circular reference error because you have included the answer cell, **A5**, in your sum range. In the general scheme of things, a company would invest any surplus cash to earn interest. On the other hand, when cash is in overdraft, it will incur interest.

If we wanted to expand our model to include this scenario, we would need to extend our cash flow statement to include interest earned or charged on the cash balance. This interest is then subtracted from or added to the existing interest charge in the profit and loss account, which changes the PAT. Since the PAT is linked to the cash flow statement, this will also result in a change in the closing cash balance, which will affect the interest earned or charged on that balance, and the cycle continues, creating a circular reference.

With each cycle or iteration, the change in the interest charged or earned on the closing cash balance of the cash flow statement gets smaller and smaller and ultimately tends toward zero. In order to create a circular reference on purpose, you need to ask Excel to allow it by going to **Options** and checking **Enable iterative calculations**. You can leave the maximum number of iterations at 100.

I do not recommend this for anyone other than expert users, and even then, only when you will not be sharing your model with other users, for the following reason:

Unfortunately, circular references, when enabled, are notoriously unreliable and can cause Excel to become unstable. When this happens, Excel populates the worksheet with errors. You would then need to spend time combing through the model to manually zero out the cells that are the source of the circularity. Alternatively, you could restore a backup that does not contain the circularity.

This can be quite alarming to all except expert users of Excel and can lead to the loss of hours of modeling time. The best way around this is to include a **circuit breaker** from the onset, as seen in the following screenshot:

	B	C	D	E	F	G	H	I	J	K	L
fx	=IF(E5="OFF".SUM*(C3:C9),0)										
		23									
		34									
		32		OFF	Circuit breaker cell						
		53			OFF or 1 = Allow circular reference; ON or 0 = Zero out circularity cells						
		=IF(E5="OFF".SUM*(C3:C9),0)									

To do this, designate an empty cell, say cell **E5**, as the circuit breaker then type in OFF or 1, to allow the circular reference; or ON or 0, to zero out the cells with circularity.

You then enclose the cell(s) containing the circular reference in an IF statement. The logical question would be E5=1. If this is true, then allow the formula with the circular reference; otherwise, set the value as 0.

The default value of the circuit breaker should be OFF; then, if the formula goes rogue, just type ON in the circuit breaker cell to trigger 0 in the IF statement and clear the circularity.

Remember that Excel continuously recalculates formula cells, so this could be a regular occurrence. Once again, this should only be done by expert users who will not be sharing their model.

Creating a quick cash flow statement

Now that you have learned how to create a cash flow statement and everything you need to do, let's go ahead and prepare a simple statement for a specific scenario. Let's assume that you are the founder of a web design company and you need to keep tabs on everything that you spend money on, because as a start-up, capital is vital to the development of the company. We will create a simple cash flow statement to track the first year of expenses, so that we can understand whether it will be profitable to proceed with the company later down the line:

1. We will begin by creating two cells at the top, with the financial year and the cash invested at the beginning of that year, as follows:

Cash Flow Statement
Financial Year
Cash at Beginning of Year

2. As we have learned in this chapter, cash flow will be divided into three main sections, the first of which is operational activities. So, let's create a table containing all of the expenses and cash influx that falls under core operations. The operational influx of the web design company will mainly be from two places:
   - Customers requesting websites
   - Freelance graphic design undertaken by employees

So, our **Cash invoices** tab will look as follows:

Cash Flow Statement		
Financial Year		
Cash at Beginning of Year		
Cash flow from core operations		
Cash invoices		
1		Customers
2		Graphic design

3. As for operational expenses, they can be categorized as follows:
    - Hosting services for websites
    - Resources needed for working on websites
    - Employee wages
    - Income taxes, and so on

After compiling all of these in a table, it should look similar to the following screenshot:

Cash Flow Statement	
Financial Year	
Cash at Beginning of Year	
Cash flow from core operations	
Cash invoices	
1	Customers
2	Graphic design
Cash expenses	
1	Hosting services
2	General operating services and rent
3	Wage expenses
4	Interest
5	Income taxes

4. Finally, we will add a net cash flow row to display the total cash flow from operations. In the cell assigned to it, we will enter the following formula:

```
=SUM(D8:D15)
```

We have now completed the operations part of our cash flow statement.

5. Now, we will create a table similar to the operations table; this time, for investing activities. In this table, we will use the following as cash invoices:
    - Sale of web domains and templates
    - Graphic design sales

So, our cash flow statement now looks similar to the following screenshot:

Cash Flow Statement		
Financial Year		
Cash at Beginning of Year		
Cash flow from core operations		
Cash invoices		
1	Customers	
2	Graphic design	
Cash expenses		
1	Hosting services	
2	General operating services and rent	
3	Wage expenses	
4	Interest	
5	Income taxes	
Net cash flow from operations		0.00
Cash flow from investing activities		
Cash invoices		
1	Sale of web domains and templates	
2	Graphic design sales	

6. Expenses for investing activities consist of the following:
   - Purchasing computers and other equipment
   - Fun activities for employees
   - Employee appreciation

We will add these into a table, as follows:

Cash Flow Statement		
Financial Year		
Cash at Beginning of Year		
Cash flow from core operations		
Cash invoices		
1	Customers	
2	Graphic design	
Cash expenses		
1	Hosting services	
2	General operating services and rent	
3	Wage expenses	
4	Interest	
5	Income taxes	
Net cash flow from operations		0.00
Cash flow from investing activities		
Cash invoices		
1	Sale of web domains and templates	
2	Graphic design sales	
Cash expenses		
1	Purchase of computers	
2	Fun activities	
3	Employee appreciation	

7. Then, similar to the operations table, we will create a row displaying the total cash flow from investing activities. So far, our cash flow statement should look as follows:

Cash Flow Statement		
Financial Year		
Cash at Beginning of Year		
Cash flow from core operations		
Cash invoices		
1	Customers	
2	Graphic design	
Cash expenses		
1	Hosting services	
2	General operating services and rent	
3	Wage expenses	
4	Interest	
5	Income taxes	
Net cash flow from operations		0.00
Cash flow from investing activities		
Cash invoices		
1	Sale of web domains and templates	
2	Graphic design sales	
Cash expenses		
1	Purchase of computers	
2	Fun activities	
3	Employee appreciation	
Net cash flow from investing activities		0.00

8. We will now repeat the same procedure for financing activities, that modifying the elements, as shown in the following screenshot:

Cash Flow Statement		
Financial Year		
Cash at Beginning of Year		
Cash flow from core operations		
Cash invoices		
1	Customers	
2	Graphic design	
Cash expenses		
1	Hosting services	
2	General operating services and rent	
3	Wage expenses	
4	Interest	
5	Income taxes	
Net cash flow from operations		0.00
Cash flow from investing activities		
Cash invoices		
1	Sale of web domains and templates	
2	Graphic design sales	
Cash expenses		
1	Purchase of computers	
2	Fun activities	
3	Employee appreciation	
Net cash flow from investing activities		0.00
Cash flow from financing activities		
Cash invoices		
1	Issuance of stock	
2	Borrowing	
Cash expenses		
1	Repurchase of stock (treasury stock)	
2	Repayment of loans	
3	Dividends	
Net cash flow from financing activities		0.00

9. Our final task is to create a cell which will display the total cash earned throughout the year after deductions, as follows:

Cash Flow Statement				Cash at the end of the year	0.00
Financial Year					
Cash at Beginning of Year					
Cash flow from core operations					
Cash invoices					
1	Customers				
2	Graphic design				
Cash expenses					
1	Hosting services				
2	General operating services and rent				
3	Wage expenses				

To calculate the total cash earned, all we need to do is find the sum of the values present in the net cash flow cells for all three activities, and the cash invested at the beginning of the year. In this case, the formula would be as follows:

```
=D16+D27+D38+D4
```

The SUM function is more useful when you have a range of numbers with no breaks in between. When adding values from different places, it is always better to use direct cell referencing.

So, our final cash flow statement looks as follows:

Cash Flow Statement		
Financial Year		
Cash at Beginning of Year		
Cash flow from core operations		
Cash invoices		
1	Customers	
2	Graphic design	
Cash expenses		
1	Hosting services	
2	General operating services and rent	
3	Wage expenses	
4	Interest	
5	Income taxes	
Net cash flow from operations	0.00	
Cash flow from investing activities		
Cash invoices		
1	Sale of web domains and templates	
2	Graphic design sales	
Cash expenses		
1	Purchase of computers	
2	Fun activities	
3	Employee appreciation	
Net cash flow from investing activities	0.00	
Cash flow from financing activities		
Cash invoices		
1	Issuance of stock	
2	Borrowing	
Cash expenses		
1	Repurchase of stock (treasury stock)	
2	Repayment of loans	
3	Dividends	
Net cash flow from financing activities	0.00	

Cash at the end of the year — 0.00

Now, we will input some values into all the required cells, and see the final cash in hand at the end of the year:

Cash Flow Statement		
For the Year Ending	31-Dec-2019	
Cash at Beginning of Year	50,000.00	
Cash flow from core operations		
Cash invoices		
1	Customers	1,500,000.00
2	Graphic design	40,000.00
Cash expenses		
1	Hosting services	(200,000.00)
2	General operating services and rent	(400,000.00)
3	Wage expenses	(300,000.00)
4	Interest	(20,000.00)
5	Income taxes	(40,000.00)
Net cash flow from operations		580,000.00
Cash flow from investing activities		
Cash invoices		
1	Sale of web domains and templates	200,000.00
2	Graphic design	30,000.00
Cash expenses		
1	Purchase of computers	(420,000.00)
2	Fun activities	(20,000.00)
3	Employee appreciation	(20,000.00)
Net cash flow from investing activities		(230,000.00)
Cash flow from financing activities		
Cash invoices		
1	Issuance of stock	0.00
2	Borrowing	0.00
Cash expenses		
1	Repurchase of stock (treasury stock)	0.00
2	Repayment of loans	400,000.00
3	Dividends	0.00
Net cash flow from financing activities		400,000.00

Cash at the end of the year 800,000.00

Hey, that's not bad! Looks like the company is doing well and is going down the right path for a start-up! We have created a simple cash flow statement that could come in handy for a lot of scenarios. The template that has been created here can be found in the GitHub repository for the book as `CashFlowCompany.xlsx`.

Summary

In this chapter, we learned how to create our cash flow statement using various functions in Excel. We learned how to factor in various elements, such as items not involving cash movement, cash flow from various activities such as investment and finance, and so on. We also learned how to balance the sheet so that everything is accurate. We also understood how to troubleshoot any errors that might occur here. Finally, we created a sample cash flow statement for a specific scenario.

In the next chapter, we will look at various kinds of ratio analysis.

8
Ratio Analysis

In order to assess a company, most people immediately look at its profit history. While this is one of the indicators that should be considered, it could be a mistake to make a decision based solely on that information. As we saw in `Chapter 7`, *Cash Flow Statement*, profits do not always equate to cash, and even the most profitable company can fold if the profits are not backed up by cash flow.

Ratio analysis looks at the profitability, liquidity, asset management and efficiency, debt management, and market value of a company. Each ratio takes two strategic items from financial statements and examines the relationship between them in order to gain some insight into the company's profitability, liquidity, and so on.

In this chapter, we will cover the following topics:

- Understanding the meaning and benefits of ratio analysis
- Learning about the various kinds of ratios
- Interpreting ratios
- Understanding the limitations of ratio analysis
- Using ratios to find financially stable companies

Understanding the meaning and benefits of ratio analysis

A ratio is calculated by dividing one item by another—for example, profit divided by turnover. However, you should not pick items from financial statements at random and divide them; you should select items whose ratio will be meaningful and provide information that will aid decision-making. In the example of profit divided by turnover, this ratio, otherwise called the profit margin, tells you how much profit is generated for every Naira of turnover.

Ratios are usually expressed as percentages, but also as percentages as they apply to **times** or **days**. A profit margin of 20% means that after all relevant deductions, the company retains 20% of its turnover as profit. In other words, the profit for the period is 20% of the turnover. The ratios on their own are useful in directing the attention of management and section heads to areas of concern; however, it would be more useful if the ratios were calculated over a period of time so that a trend could be established.

This is particularly true for the company's external interest groups, such as investors. Management has access to other internal information not available to third parties and can therefore extract more meaning from ratios for the year. Investors only have access to the published financial statements. Ratios, which are prepared from the financial statements, are therefore of particular significance to investors and other external interest groups. The ratios should be calculated over a number of years in order to ensure that the results are a true reflection of the company's performance. The results can then be compared to similar companies and the norm for the industry in which the company operates. They can also be used as a basis for forecasting.

Learning about the various kinds of ratios

There are thousands of ratios, and you could easily get carried away with them. To make life easier for us, ratios can be classified under five broad categories—namely, profitability, liquidity, efficiency, debt management, and market ratios.

We will examine a few examples for each of these categories.

These ratios measure how capable a company is of converting turnover into profit. These ratios are usually referred to as the **margin**, which generally means that they are divided by turnover. Let's look at the gross profit margin, which is expressed as the following formula:

$$\frac{\text{Gross Profit \%}}{\text{Turnover}}$$

Here, the gross profit is the turnover less the cost of sales.

Sometimes, when a company makes a loss, you can still take some comfort if there is a gross profit. This means that the direct costs have been covered and there is some contribution towards overheads or administrative expenses. The gross profit margin will tend to be fairly constant over the years, as it often reflects the company's markup policy. If the gross profit margin (or simply the gross margin) is very low, or even negative, then it is fair to conclude that the company is in trouble. This ratio is of particular importance to management, which sets the mark-up policy of the company.

There are other categories of profit whose margin can be calculated. The relevance of the profit margins will depend on which interest group you belong to. Providers of debt expect repayment of the principal debt plus interest. They will therefore be interested in the profit before interest, referred to as earnings before interest and tax, or EBIT. The EBIT margin is expressed as the following formula:

$$\frac{EBIT\%}{Turnover}$$

The higher the margin, the more confident investors will be, as the margin indicates that the company can repay principal and interest as they fall due. Equity holders, such as shareholders, are the last to be considered for the distribution of a company's profits. Only after depreciation, interest, and taxation do you arrive at the profit available for distribution. Equity holders will therefore be particularly interested in profit after tax, or PAT.

The PAT margin is expressed as the following formula:

$$\frac{PAT\%}{Turnover}$$

EBITDA is popular among some analysts as they feel that it allows the user to observe the company's performance before it is influenced by CapEx policy, in the form of depreciation and debt appetite, such as interest and government policy.

Earnings before interest, taxation, depreciation, and amortization (EBITDA) is therefore considered a purer indicator of a company's financial health.

The EBITDA margin is expressed as the following formula:

$$\frac{EBITDA\%}{Turnover}$$

Liquidity ratios

Liquidity is one of the most important indicators of whether a company will be able to meet its obligations as they fall due—in other words, whether it is a going concern. Liquidity ratios compare a company's current assets with its current liabilities. If short-term liabilities are not sufficiently covered by short-term assets, that is the first sign we that need to take action to prevent the company from becoming distressed.

The current ratio is expressed as follows:

$$\frac{\text{Current Assets}}{\text{Current Liabilities}}$$

It is difficult to specify what figure represents a good ratio; however, a current ratio of 1.5 to 2 is generally considered to be adequate. A much lower figure would indicate that the company may be struggling to meets its liabilities.

On the other hand, a very high ratio would indicate that cash is being tied up that could be used to earn income. Current assets are made up broadly of the inventory, trade receivables, and cash. The quick ratio recognizes that the inventory is not as readily convertible to cash as the other current assets and compares the current assets minus the inventory with current liabilities.

The quick ratio is expressed as follows:

$$\frac{\text{Current Assets - Inventory}}{\text{Current Liabilities}}$$

The strictest test of liquidity is the acid test, which compares the cash with the current liabilities.

The acid test is expressed as follows:

$$\frac{\text{Cash}}{\text{Current Liabilities}}$$

Efficiency ratios

Efficiency ratios measure how well a company utilizes its assets and manages its liabilities in order to generate income.

The following are some examples of efficiency ratios:

- **Inventory days**: The average inventory is obtained by taking the average of the opening and closing inventory. The daily cost of goods sold is obtained by dividing the cost of goods sold for the year by 365. The result is expressed in days and represents the amount of time inventory stays before it is sold. The company should keep enough stock to satisfy customer demand without delays; however, keeping too much stock or holding on to stock for too long will lead to additional costs. Management will have to find a balance between the two. This ratio is calculated as follows:

$$\frac{\text{Average Inventory}}{\text{Daily Cost of Goods Sold}}$$

- **Accounts receivable (debtor) days**: The average accounts receivable is obtained by taking the average of the opening and closing accounts receivable. Daily sales are obtained by dividing sales for the year by 365. The result is expressed in days and represents the amount of time it takes customers to pay for goods bought from the company on credit. Management needs to give customers enough time to pay for goods and services in order to encourage them to continue doing business with the company; however, the credit terms should not be too liberal as this could result in cash-flow problems. This is calculated as follows:

$$\frac{\text{Average Accounts Receivable}}{\text{Daily Credit Sales}}$$

- **Accounts payable (creditor) days**: The average accounts payable is obtained by taking the average of the opening and closing accounts payable. The daily cost of goods sold is obtained by dividing the cost of goods sold for the year by 365. The result is expressed in days and represents the amount of time it takes the company to pay for goods bought from suppliers on credit. Management should aim to take as much time as possible, without alienating its suppliers, to pay for credit purchases. This is calculated as follows:

$$\frac{\text{Average Accounts Payable}}{\text{Daily Cost of Goods Sold}}$$

Return on average assets

Return on average assets (ROAA) compares the profit realized in the year to the average total assets during the year. It is a measure of how efficiently the company has utilized its assets to generate profit.

The ROAA is calculated as follows:

$$\frac{\text{EBIT \%}}{\text{Average Total Assets}}$$

From this formula, we come to know that the EBIT is the earnings or profit before interest and tax, and the average total assets is the average of the opening and closing total assets. This is a very important ratio as it gives context to some of the profitability ratios.

Consider the following screenshot of an ROAA:

	Company A	Company B
	N	N
Turnover	20,000,000	10,000,000
EBIT	2,000,000	1,000,000
Opening Total Assets	80,000,000	15,000,000
Closing Total Assets	100,000,000	30,000,000
Average Total Assets	90,000,000	22,500,000
Return on Total Assets	2.2%	4.4%

At first glance, company A appears to be the more attractive with double the turnover and double the EBIT; however, a closer look shows that company A has utilized assets of N90 million to generate a profit of N2 million, while company B has generated a profit of N1 million with assets of only N22.5 million.

In other words, company B has been more efficient in the use of its assets, giving a return on average assets of 4.4% compared to only 2.2% by company A.

Return on average capital employed

Return on average capital employed (**ROACE**): This ratio determines how efficiently a company utilizes its capital. It is calculated as follows:

$$ROCE = \frac{EBIT\ \%}{Average\ Capital\ Employed}$$

The phrase **capital employed** refers to the debt and equity capital, and can be calculated as follows:

$$Capital\ Employed = Total\ Assets - Current\ Liabilities$$

This is one of the most popular ratios and is used to compare how economically different companies utilize their capital. The higher the ROACE, the more efficiently capital is employed. There is no absolute figure that you should target for ROACE, and as with other ratios, it is more meaningful when calculated over time; however, you would expect the ROACE to be higher than the cost of capital.

Return on average equity

Return on average equity (**ROAE**): This is calculated as follows:

$$ROE = \frac{PAT\ \%}{Average\ Equity}$$

In the preceding equation, PAT refers to the profit after tax. The ratio uses the net income or PAT rather than the EBIT, since interest and tax have to be paid before arriving at the profit attributable to the equity holders.

Rearranging the accounting equation *Assets = Liabilities + Equity*, you get *Equity = Assets – Liabilities*.

This is an alternative way of determining equity. Return on equity measures how efficiently and profitably the company uses its equity capital.

Debt-management ratios

Debt-management ratios measure the long-term solvency of a company. The following are some debt-management ratios:

- **Leverage or debt to equity**: This ratio measures the extent to which a company depends on debt financing as opposed to equity financing. The higher the ratio, the more dependent the company is on external debt. A highly leveraged company must ensure that it meets the expectations of long-term debt holders to keep them from calling in their debts early, which could cripple the company. This is calculated as follows:

$$\text{Leverage} = \frac{\text{Debt}}{\text{Equity}}$$

- **Interest cover**: This ratio measures whether the company is generating enough profit to comfortably cover the cost of external debt and interest. This is calculated as follows:

$$\text{Interest cover} = \frac{\text{EBIT}}{\text{Interest}}$$

- **Market value ratios:** Earnings per share is a widely used ratio to calculate market value, and is calculated as follows:

$$\text{Earnings Per Share (EPS)} = \frac{\text{Profit After Tax}}{\text{No. of Ordinary Shares}}$$

If there are preference shares, preference dividends will be deducted from the PAT before dividing it by the number of ordinary shares. The EPS ratio can also be classed as a profitability ratio. It is being mentioned here because it is a popular market indicator of how much of a company's profit is retained for each ordinary share.

- **Price earnings ratio:** The P/E ratio is a measure of how much investors are willing to pay for the company's profit or earnings. This is calculated as follows:

$$\text{Price to Earnings (P/E) ratio} = \frac{\text{Market Price}}{\text{Earnings per Share}}$$

Interpreting ratios

The investors and other external interest groups of a company usually only have access to the financial statements of the company. However, financial details alone are of limited use when trying to assess a company. Ratios are a valuable tool for such interest groups, giving them the opportunity to assess companies in a standardized manner using widely accepted parameters.

It is usually a very subjective process to try and compare companies of different sizes, geographical locations, fiscal jurisdictions, and nature. Ratio analysis provides a level playing field by laying emphasis on performance rather than absolute size of turnover or profit. Efficiency, profitability, and liquidity are more or less independent of the absolute size of the individual parameters involved, such as turnover, assets, profit, and liabilities.

Ratio analysis allows the comparison of diverse companies, and also allows analysts to set benchmarks for the different ratios so that up-and-coming companies can assess their performance against these benchmarks and identify areas where they need to improve, as well as those areas where they are doing well.

Management can use ratio analysis to monitor the performance of department heads. They could use it to set targets and thresholds for rewards or bonuses. If ratios are calculated over several periods, they may reveal a trend that could highlight impending difficulties that can then be addressed before they crystallize.

We will now look at some examples of different kinds of trend analysis.

An increase in the gross profit percentage is not necessarily a good thing. You would have to consider the following:

- Ensure that the increase is not a result of some error, such as the overstatement of turnover or the understatement of the cost of sales.
- Find out whether this is a result of a change in company policy.
- Observe what effect this has had on the volume of sales. The increased gross profit percentage may have resulted in the loss of market share.

If this loss in market share continues unchecked, it could affect the company's ability to continue in business. Management could decide to reduce the markup on their products in order to attract customers back to their products and eventually restore their market share. A decrease in gross profit percentage is not necessarily a bad thing. You would have to consider the following:

- Ensure that the decrease is not a result of some error, such as the understatement of turnover or the overstatement of the cost of sales.
- Find out whether this is a result of a change in company policy.
- Observe what effect this has had on the volume of sales. The decreased gross profit percentage may have resulted in an increase of the market share, which will translate to increased profit.

Another example of interpreting ratios concerns liquidity ratios. A high current ratio indicates a healthy company with respect to liquidity; however, the quick ratio will reveal how much this liquidity depends on inventory. If the quick ratio drops drastically, with the exclusion of inventory from the equation, then management will need to look at ways of reducing the dependence on inventory to reflect liquidity.

One way of doing this is to reduce the amount of cash tied up in the inventory. As long as it does not affect the ability to satisfy customers' demands, management may consider holding less inventory. Another way to improve liquidity is to try and boost turnover, which will filter through to debtors and/or cash. Even if creditors also increase the company's markup, this will ensure that there is a net improvement in liquidity.

The acid test, which compares just the cash with the current liabilities, is a worst-case scenario ratio. It would only become relevant if a large creditor suddenly made an enforceable demand on what the company owes them.

Some ways to guard against this are as follows:

- Avoid depending on just one supplier. Where possible, spread your exposure over a number of suppliers so that if one supplier begins to apply pressure for quick settlement of outstanding balances, the company can quickly shift focus onto the other suppliers.
- Be prudent in selecting suppliers. A supplier that has a history of suddenly making demands on their balances should be avoided.

- Management should adopt a know-your-supplier policy. The health of all suppliers should be monitored so that at the first sign that a supplier is experiencing problems and may have to demand the quick settlement of their balances, the company can take appropriate action to reduce the dependence on that supplier.
- Management should ensure that inventory and debtors are being efficiently converted into cash.

Understanding the limitations of ratio analysis

It is important to realize that ratios do not actually solve any problems; they merely highlight trends and exceptions that can then be acted upon. Definitions of ratios often vary from one analyst to another—for example, the quick ratio and the acid test. Some analysts refer to the ratio of current assets minus inventory divided by current liabilities as the quick ratio, while others refer to the same ratio as the acid test.

One school of thought uses the year-end balances for assets in ROA and equity and long-term debt in ROACE. Another school of thought recognizes that companies can manipulate this ratio by posting significant transactions at the year end, only to reverse them in the new year. They therefore use the average of those balances that will counter such practices. These differences in approach can lead to vastly different results. Another criticism of ratio analysis is that it uses historical values and does not take into account changes in market value.

Finally, ratio analysis, by its nature, only looks at quantitative results, the monetary implications of the ratios, and trends. An assessment of a company cannot be complete without considering qualitative features, such as social responsibility, business model, market share, quality of management, and effect of operations on the environment.

Now that we know about the various ratios, let's try to apply them to real-life scenarios.

Using ratios to find financially stable companies

Let's assume that you are looking to invest in a company that is financially stable and has a good market value. We can find out the best company for this using the following ratios:

- **EPS**: This can be useful ratio for finding the best company to invest in because it shows you how much money the company makes as profit for each share that the company sells
- **P/E ratio**: This ratio tells you that there might be more growth in the future of the company, and it also shows you how much an investor is willing to pay for a share

We will go through the following steps to use these ratios:

1. Open the `CompanyInvestment.xlsx` file, where you will find details about some companies, such as their PAT, number of shares, and the market price of each share, as shown in the following screenshot:

Company stocks in FY19					
	PAT	No of Shares	Market price of a share	EPS	P/E Ratio
Company 1	202351	500,000	$50.00		
Company 2	284001	300,000	$28.00		
Company 3	369541	450,000	$11.00		
Company 4	137870	100,000	$90.00		
Company 5	185350	125,000	$18.00		

2. Now, we will calculate the EPS for each company by dividing the PAT with the `No of Shares` of each company, using cell referencing, as follows:

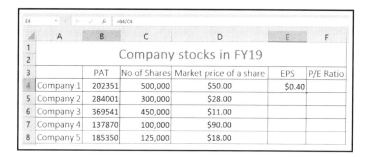

We can see from this that `Company 1` earns `0.40$` per share.

3. Now, we will calculate the same thing for all the other companies by double-clicking on the fill handle so that we can see the EPS for all the companies, as follows:

Company stocks in FY19					
	PAT	No of Shares	Market price of a share	EPS	P/E Ratio
Company 1	202351	500,000	$50.00	$0.40	
Company 2	284001	300,000	$28.00	$0.95	
Company 3	369541	450,000	$11.00	$0.82	
Company 4	137870	100,000	$90.00	$1.38	
Company 5	185350	125,000	$18.00	$1.48	

We can see that Company 5 has the highest EPS and will be more profitable for investors in the long run.

4. Now, we will calculate the P/E ratio for each company. For Company 1, we can do this by dividing the market price of its share by the EPS of that company, as follows:

	A	B	C	D	E	F
				=D4/E4		
1			Company stocks in FY19			
2						
3		PAT	No of Shares	Market price of a share	EPS	P/E Ratio
4	Company 1	202351	500,000	$50.00	$0.40	124
5	Company 2	284001	300,000	$28.00	$0.95	
6	Company 3	369541	450,000	$11.00	$0.82	
7	Company 4	137870	100,000	$90.00	$1.38	
8	Company 5	185350	125,000	$18.00	$1.48	

We can see that the company has a really high P/E ratio of around 124! This means that there is a high chance of the company growing even more in the coming years.

5. Finally, we will find the P/E ratio for all the companies. Your table should look similar to the following:

Company stocks in FY19					
	PAT	No of Shares	Market price of a share	EPS	P/E Ratio
Company 1	202351	500,000	$50.00	$0.40	124
Company 2	284001	300,000	$28.00	$0.95	30
Company 3	369541	450,000	$11.00	$0.82	13
Company 4	137870	100,000	$90.00	$1.38	65
Company 5	185350	125,000	$18.00	$1.48	12

We can see that Company 1 is the best bet when it comes to investing, and that Company 4 is a good middle ground for investing in.

Summary

In this chapter, we have learned about the importance of ratio analysis. We have seen that there are thousands of ratios, but we have learned that not all will be relevant in any given situation. We looked at how to identify the five main groups of ratios and worked through examples from all five groups.

In the next chapter, we will look at absolute (by discounted cash flow) and relative (by comparative measurements) methods of valuation. We will cover the concept of the time value of money and use it extensively in our calculations. We will learn about several concepts, including free cash flow, the weighted average cost of capital, and terminal value, among others.

9
Valuation

Whatever the reason for establishing and running a company, you will, at some stage, want to know the value of the business. This could be because of one of the following reasons:

- To identify weaknesses
- To determine whether the business is growing, stagnant, or deteriorating
- To apply for a loan
- To attract investors
- To establish a reference point as a platform for driving future growth
- In preparation for divesting from the company

There are several methods of valuation, but the three main methods will be discussed in this chapter.

This chapter will cover the following topics:

- Absolute valuation
- Relative valuation
- Interpreting the results

Absolute valuation

It is widely accepted that the most accurate way to value an enterprise is by absolute valuation using the **discounted cash flow (DCF)** method. Crucially, this method considers the time value of money. It also considers the cash flow throughout the projected life of the enterprise. This adheres closely to the definition of an enterprise's worth as the total amount of cash flow it can generate.

The DCF method includes technical concepts and calculations. We will attempt to simplify those concepts, but nevertheless, you will not have to repeat most of the complex computations required to derive some of the parameters necessary for the valuation. There will always be resources available for you to refer to, and you will certainly create your own database of resources, which you can tap as required.

Free cash flow

The DCF method continues from where the 3-statement method ends. It begins with the concept of **free cash flow** or **FCF**. The goal is to determine the cash flow generated by the company; however, you need to recognize that some of the cash generated is committed **inter alia** to satisfying the debt holders and capital expenditure plans. We will therefore need to adjust the cash generated for these items in order to arrive at the FCF. Generally, you would calculate the free cash flow to the firm or enterprise as a whole (FCFF) and adjust this to arrive at the figure of the free cash flow to the equity holders (FCFE).

The first, FCFF, will lead us to the **enterprise value** (EV) and the second, FCFE, will lead us to the share price for the company's ordinary shares. Much like the cash flow statement, you will start with the operating profit, **earnings before interest and tax** (EBIT). As taxation by the government is an obligation, you need to deduct taxation at the ruling tax rate.

You then add back items that do not involve the movement of funds, such as depreciation. An increase in working capital signifies a net outflow of cash that should be deducted. If it shows a decrease in working capital, signifying a net inflow of cash, then that should be added to your total. Finally, deduct any planned **capital expenditure** (CapEx) and increase in **work in progress** (WIP) to arrive at the figure of the free cash flow to the firm, the FCFF.

When a company undertakes a project to build or construct a fixed asset, the project sometimes extends beyond the year end. Since, at that stage, the project is not yet complete, it would be misleading to allocate the costs incurred so far to the asset account. The normal practice is to create a WIP account and post all expenditure on unfinished projects to that account. As soon as the projects are concluded, the balance on the account is transferred to the appropriate property, plant and equipment, or fixed asset account.

The following screenshot shows the calculation of an FCFF forecast for five years:

	A	B	C	J	K	L	M	N
1								
2	*(Unless otherwise specified, all financials are*			Y06F	Y07F	Y08F	Y09F	Y10F
3								
4	**DCF Valuation using FCFF**							
5								
6	EBIT			55,658	66,822	78,542	90,844	103,754
7	Tax Rate (%)							
8	EBIT*(1-t)			38,961	46,776	54,980	63,591	72,628
9	Add: Depreciation			30,000	30,000	30,000	30,000	30,000
10	Change in Working Capital			(15,107)	12,028	(15,245)	11,883	(15,396)
11	Less: Capex and increase in WIP			-	-	-	-	-
12	**Free Cashflow to the Firm (FCFF)**			53,854	88,803	69,734	105,474	87,232

Time value of money

In Chapter 1, *Introduction to Financial Modeling and Excel*, we were introduced to the concept of the time value of money. Money in your hand today could be potentially worth more than the same funds a year from now. This is because you could invest those funds and in a year's time, you could receive them back along with interest; N1,000 invested at 10% would give you back N1,100 in a year's time, as shown in the following calculation:

$$1,000 + (1,000 \times 10\%) = 1,100$$
$$\text{Year1 cash} + 10\% \text{ of Year1 cash} = \text{Year2 cash}$$

For example, if $M1$ represents Year1 cash, r represents the interest rate, and $M2$ represents Year2 cash, then the formula becomes the following:

$$M2 = M1 + (M1 \times r)$$
$$M2 = M1 \times (1 + r)$$

Conversely, N1,100 discounted back to today would be worth N1,000.

Rearranging the previous equation, we get the following:

$$M1 = M2 \times \frac{1}{(1+r)}$$

In other words, cash today equals cash tomorrow multiplied by a discount factor.

In the preceding screenshot, the discount factor after the first year is as follows:

$$\frac{1}{1+r}$$

After the second year, the discount factor is as follows:

$$\frac{1}{(1+r)} \times \frac{1}{1+r} = [\frac{1}{(1+r)}]^2$$

After the third year, it is as follows:

$$\frac{1}{(1+r)} \times \frac{1}{1+r} \times \frac{1}{1+r} = [\frac{1}{(1+r)}]^3$$

This leads us to a discount factor after year n of the following:

$$[\frac{1}{(1+r)}]^n$$

We have forecast our free cash flows for five years into the future and obtained monetary values for each of those years' cash flows.

We now need to discount those cash flows back to today's value before we obtain an aggregate of the discounted cash flows to arrive at the enterprise value.

 Note that today is the beginning of the year FY06, the first of the forecast years.

Weighted average cost of capital

For the DCF model, the **weighted average cost of capital** (**WACC**) is **r** in the discount factor formula. A company typically has different sources of capital, debt, and equity, with each source having its own cost or expectation of the company. For example, the cost of debt capital would be the interest charge. This interest is a charge against the profit for the year, which, along with other allowable expenses, reduces the amount of profit subject to tax.

So, while the interest is the cost of the debt capital to be adjusted from our cash flow, there is an amount of tax saved when we charge the interest against profit. The tax saved by the interest expense is recognized by using the after-tax cost of capital, which is arrived at as follows:

$$\text{Cost of debt} \times (1 - \text{tax rate})$$

WACC is the average cost of the different types of capital owned by the company. The contribution of each source of capital to the WACC is weighted to account for the fraction of the overall capital it represents.

For example, if the debt-to-equity ratio is 2:1, then the cost of debt will have double the effect on the overall capital as the cost of equity and the weight of the cost of debt in WACC will reflect this, as shown in the following formula:

$$\text{WACC} = (\text{Cost of debt} \times \text{Weight of Debt}) + (\text{Cost of Equity} \times \text{Weight of Equity})$$

This equation is widely referred to as the **capital asset pricing model (CAPM)**. We have seen that the cost of debt is the interest due to the debt holders. Calculating the cost of equity is a more complex exercise. Equity carries more risk than debt, and equity holders therefore have a higher expectation of reward. Debt holders are assured of their interest as long as the company is a going concern. Equity holders have to rely on ordinary dividends, which may or may not be declared.

The cost of equity is arrived at as follows:

$$\text{Cost of Equity} = Rf + \text{Premium}$$

In the preceding formula, *Rf* is the risk-free rate. The rate for government securities is usually taken as the risk-free rate:

$$\text{The premium} = \beta \times (Rm - Rf)$$

In the preceding formula, *Rm* is the premium for the entire stock market and β is the volatility or risk of the company's shares compared to the market. So, the premium can be said to be the difference between the market premium over the risk-free rate, adjusted to accommodate the specific volatility of the company's shares compared to the market.

A β value of 1.0 signifies that the shares exactly match market volatility. For every 1% movement in the market, the shares will also move by 1% in the same direction. A higher β value signifies that the shares are more volatile than the market; they carry more risk but also more reward than the market.

A lower β value signifies that the shares are less volatile than the market, while a negative β value indicates negative correlation with the market. In other words, when the market price increases, the share price will decrease, and vice versa.

The following screenshot shows the equation and the parameters required to calculate the cost of equity and the WACC:

14	Risk free rate	8.0%	
15	Beta	0.70	
16	Expected return from market	15.0%	
17	Cost of equity	12.9%	⬅ **RFR + BETA * (MR-RFR)**
18	Cost of debt	10.0%	
19	Post tax cost of debt	7.0%	
20	Target debt: capital ratio	40.0%	
21	**WACC**	10.5%	⬅ **cost of equity * Wt + cost of debt * wt**
22			
23	Terminal Growth Rate	5.0%	

Terminal value

In your model, you have projected figures for the next five years. However, the company does not cease to exist at the end of five years but continues to generate income for the foreseeable future. The DCF method attempts to quantify all future cash flows using the concept of a **terminal value**.

At the end of the projected five years, it is assumed that the company has reached a position of stability and will continue to experience stable growth for the rest of its existence. The rate of this stable growth is called the **terminal growth rate (TGR)**. With this assumption, formulas can be drawn up to simulate the growth to infinity and then mathematically rearranged to arrive at a terminal value that represents the sum of all future cash flows, starting from the end of the fifth projected year and stretching into perpetuity.

The equation for the terminal value is as follows:

$$\text{Terminal value} = \frac{(1 + TGR)}{(WACC - TGR)}$$

The terminal value is typically the largest contributing factor to the valuation of the DCF and tends to ensure that the value obtained using this method is usually higher than the valuation reached by other methods.

The following screenshot shows the calculation of the terminal value:

	A	B	C	D	I	J	K	L	M	N
1										
2		(Unless otherwise specified, all financials are in N '000)			Y05F	Y06F	Y07F	Y08F	Y09F	Y10F
3										
4		**DCF Valuation using FCFF**								
10		Change in Working Capital				(15,107)	12,028	(15,245)	11,883	(15,396)
11		Less: Capex and increase in WIP				-	-	-	-	-
12		**Free Cashflow to the Firm (FCFF)**				53,854	88,803	69,734	105,474	87,232
13										
14		Risk free rate		8.0%						
15		Beta		0.70						
16		Expected return from market		15.0%						
17		Cost of equity		12.9%						
18		Cost of debt		10.0%						
19		Post tax cost of debt		7.0%						
20		Target debt: capital ratio		40.0%						
21		**WACC**		10.5%						
22										
23		Terminal Growth Rate	5.0%	5.0%						
24										
25		**Terminal Value**				FINAL YEAR FCFF * (1+TGR)/(WACC-TGR) ⟹				1,653,309

Calculating the present value

Using the WACC as r, you now discount the cash flows for the projected five years and the terminal value to arrive at the present values for the cash flow of each year and the terminal value.

The discount factor for year 1 is expressed as follows:

$$\frac{1}{(1+r)} = \frac{1}{(1+\mathrm{WACC})}$$

From the preceding screenshot, we can see that the WACC is 10.5%. Here, we will substitute the values for WACC:

$$\text{Discount factor for Year 1} = \frac{1}{(1+10\%)} = 0.90$$

The present value of FCFF for year 1 is as follows:

$$\text{FCFF for Year 1} = \text{FCFF (For Year 1)} \times \text{discount factor for Year 1}$$

The FCFF for Y06F, which is year 1 of our estimated years, is N53,854, as shown in the preceding screenshot. We discount this with the discount factor for year 1, 0.90:

$$53,854 \times 0.90 = 48,719$$

To give N('000) 48,719, which is the present value of the FCFF for year 1, we should perform the following calculation:

Present value of FCFF for year 2

$$= \text{FCFF Year 2} \times [\frac{1}{(1 + \text{WACC})}]^2$$

$$= 88,803 \times [\frac{1}{(1 + 10\%)}]^2$$

$$= 88,803 \times 0.82$$

$$= 72,676$$

We repeat this format to obtain the present values of the FCFF for each of the estimated years and the terminal value, as shown in the following screenshot. The discount factor for the terminal value will be the same as for the final estimated year, Y10E.

The calculation of the present values is shown in the following screenshot:

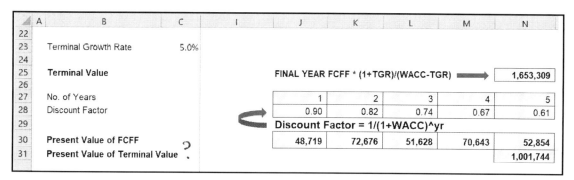

The **enterprise value (EV)** is the sum of the present values of all future cash flows:

Present Value of FCFF		48,719	72,676	51,628	70,643	52,854
Present Value of Terminal Value						1,001,744
Enterprise Value	1,298,264					

In order to get the equity value, you need to pay off the debt holders.

You do this by deducting the **net debt** (debt - cash) and any contingencies from the **Enterprise Value**, as shown in the following screenshot:

You then divide the **Equity Value** by the number of shares to arrive at the **Share Price (NAIRA)**, which is **117.2** per share.

Relative valuation – comparative company analysis

Relative valuation relies on the theory that, in general, similar companies will produce similar results. This may be a bit simplistic, but in a discipline that involves a lot of assumptions and estimates, relative valuation is popular among analysts as it provides a way to arrive at the value of a business that is plausible, quick, and simple. The actual calculations are simple and straightforward; the difficulty is in identifying comparable companies.

The main criteria to consider are as follows:

- Industry
- Size
- Capital structure
- Geographical location
- Growth rate

Industry: With reference to your major source of income, identify the appropriate industry to which the company belongs and look for examples within that industry class.

Size: The relationship between size and profits is not exactly linear. A company with twice the asset base will not necessarily make twice as much profit. There may be economies of scale and access-restricted benefits as a result of its size. Large companies will have access to volume discounts and favorable business terms not available to smaller companies in the same industry. You should therefore look for companies that are similar in size.

Capital structure: A company that relies heavily on debt puts its shareholders at greater risk. This is because debt holders must always be settled before equity holders—for example, in the event of bankruptcy. In addition, companies that are heavily geared will have to maintain a healthy interest cover ratio in order to maintain their creditworthiness. You should look for companies with similar debt-to-equity ratios.

Geographical location: This is very important as location can have a significant effect on a company's operations. The economic climate, tax, tariffs, and other relevant legislation could differ, and this could have a significant effect on the bottom line. You should look for companies within the same geographical location.

Growth rate: A company that grows fast will be more attractive to potential investors than one with a slower growth rate. You should therefore look for companies with a similar growth rate. It will be impossible to find companies that meet all these criteria, and therefore you will have to use your own judgement to select those that are most similar to the company you are modeling. Once you have identified four or five companies, you will then need to obtain a number of multiples, which will be used in your comparative valuation.

The most common multiples used for this purpose are as follows:

- EV/Sales—Enterprise value by Sales
- EV/EBITDA—Enterprise value by EBITDA
- P/E—Price-to-earnings ratio

The idea is that similar companies will have similar multiples. So, if *EV/Sales=K* for company A, then the same multiple for a similar company, company B, will also be = *K*.

Taking company A:

$$EV / Sales = K$$

Taking *Sales* to the right-hand side to isolate *EV*, we get the following:

$$EV = K \times Sales$$

So, once we have *Sales* for company B, we can calculate *EV* by adopting the same multiple, *K* from company A.

In practice, the multiples for four or five similar companies you identify will never be exactly the same, so you will take the mean (average) or median as the common multiple, *K*.

Trading comparatives

The following is a screenshot of the trading multiples of five similar companies; it shows the relevant parameters required for valuation by trading comparatives, set out in tabular form:

Trading Comparatives					
Company	EV	Mkt Cap	EV/ Sales	EV/ EBITDA	P/ E (x)
			FY06F	FY06F	FY06F
Company A	2,141.0	2,670.3	2.4x	9.1x	18.2x
Company B	1,321.0	3,385.8	2.3x	10.3x	22.1x
Company C	1,456.0	3,623.4	3.1x	11.3x	23.7x
Company D	1,289.0	3,866.4	1.9x	10.1x	21.4x
Company E	987.0	2,970.0	2.2x	9.3x	15.1x
Mean			2.4x	10.0x	20.1x
Median			2.3x	10.1x	21.4x

Mkt Cap is the market capitalization, which is the total naira value of the ordinary shares of the company. The mean and median of the multiples are taken. Usually, the median is used in order to remove the effect of outliers. If you had a set of figures that read 3, 5, 4, 3, and 22, then the mean (or average) would be 7 and the median 4. Looking at this set, the number 22 is clearly an outlier; for one reason or another, it is much larger than the other members of the set. It has clearly influenced the mean to return a figure, 7, which does not appear to be in line with the other numbers in the set.

The median, however, by its nature, has neutralized the effect of the outlier and returned a figure, 4, which is more representative of the set as a whole.

The following screenshot shows the medians of the selected multiples that are used to calculate a share price for the company:

Trading Comparatives

Company	EV	Mkt Cap	EV/ Sales	EV/ EBITDA	P/ E (x)
			FY06F	FY06F	FY06F
Company A	2,141.0	2,670.3	2.4x	9.1x	18.2x
Company B	1,321.0	3,385.8	2.3x	10.3x	22.1x
Company C	1,456.0	3,623.4	3.1x	11.3x	23.7x
Company D	1,289.0	3,866.4	1.9x	10.1x	21.4x
Company E	987.0	2,970.0	2.2x	9.3x	15.1x
Mean			2.4x	10.0x	20.1x
Median			2.3x	10.1x	21.4x

	Multiple (x)	Sales	EV	Net Debt	Mkt Cap	Share Price
FY06F EV/ Sales (x)	2.3x	325,582	748,838	126,694	622,144	62.2
	(Median)					

	Multiple (x)	EBITDA	EV	Net Debt	Mkt Cap	Share Price
FY06F EV/ EBITDA (x)	10.1x	58,908	594,971	126,694	468,277	46.8
	(Median)					

	Multiple (x)	PAT	Mkt Cap	Share Price
FY06F P/ E (x)	21.4x	20,236	433,042	43.3

For the EV/Sales multiple, the equation is as follows:

$$\frac{EV}{Sales} = \text{Multiple}$$
$$\therefore EV = \text{Sales} \times \text{Multiple}$$

The median for the EV/Sales multiple is **2.3**.

The sales for the company you are reviewing total a figure of **325,582**. So, our EV for this company is as follows:

$$\therefore EV = 325,582 \times 2.3$$
$$EV = 748,838$$

To get the equity value, we need to deduct the net debt of **126,694** to get the market capitalization:

$$Equity = 748,838 - 126,694 = 622,144$$

The number of shares is 100 million, so our share price becomes the following:

$$\therefore Share\ price = 622,144/100,000,000 \times 10^3$$
$$\therefore Share\ price = N62.2$$

EBITDA for the company you are reviewing is 58,908. Using EV/EBITDA, the equation is as follows:

$$\therefore EV = 58,908 \times 10.1$$
$$EV = 594,971$$

To get the equity value, we need to deduct the net debt of **126,694** to get the market capitalization:

$$Equity = 594,971 - 126,695 = 468,277$$

The number of shares is 100 million, so the share price will become the following:

$$\therefore Share\ price = 468,277/100,000,000 \times 10^3$$
$$\therefore Share\ price = N46.8$$

Using the P/E ratio in the same way, we get the share price of **N43.3**, as shown in the preceding screenshot.

Precedent transaction comparative

The precedent transaction comparative method looks at similar companies that have recently undertaken similar transactions and assumes the price at which the securities changed hands.

The following screenshot shows a table of similar transactions with their multiples:

Transaction Comparatives

Transaction	Year	EV/sales (x)	EV/EBITDA (x)	P/E (x)	% stake
Acquisition	FY03	2.7x	11.7x	23.0x	100.0%
Acquisition	FY03	1.5x	7.2x	13.3x	60.0%
Investment	FY03	3.0x	10.0x	17.5x	22.0%
Investment	FY02	1.8x	5.9x	11.7x	10.0%
Investment	FY01	2.8x	12.2x	19.5x	35.0%
Mean		**2.4x**	**9.4x**	**17.0x**	
Median		**2.7x**	**10.0x**	**17.5x**	

The share price computations are shown in the following screenshot:

Trading Comparatives

Company	EV	Mkt Cap	EV/ Sales	EV/ EBITDA	P/ E (x)	
			FY06F	FY06F	FY06F	
Company A	2,141.0	2,670.3	2.4x	9.1x	18.2x	
Company B	1,321.0	3,385.8	2.3x	10.3x	22.1x	
Company C	1,456.0	3,623.4	3.1x	11.3x	23.7x	
Company D	1,289.0	3,866.4	1.9x	10.1x	21.4x	
Company E	987.0	2,970.0	2.2x	9.3x	15.1x	
Mean			**2.4x**	**10.0x**	**20.1x**	
Median			**2.3x**	**10.1x**	**21.4x**	

	Multiple (x)	Sales	EV	Net Debt	Mkt Cap	Share Price
FY06F EV/ Sales (x)	2.3x	325,582	748,838	126,694	622,144	62.2
	(Median)					

	Multiple (x)	EBITDA	EV	Net Debt	Mkt Cap	Share Price
FY06F EV/ EBITDA (x)	10.1x	58,908	594,971	126,694	468,277	46.8
	(Median)					

	Multiple (x)	PAT	Mkt Cap	Share Price
FY06F P/ E (x)	21.4x	20,236	433,042	43.3

Using EV/Sales, the share price is N75.2.

Using EV/EBITDA, the share price is N46.2.

Using P/E ratio, the share price is N35.4.

A summary of the results is shown in the following screenshot:

Summary of Results		
Method	**Lowest (N)**	**Highest (N)**
DCF	117.2	117.2
Trading Comparatives	43.3	62.2
Transaction Comarativ	35.4	75.2

We can represent these results in a **football field chart**. The chart gets its nickname from the way the different values obtained are scattered around the chart like football players on a football field.

In order to plot the chart, we create a table showing the minimum and maximum values for the share price obtained for each method and multiple, as well as the difference between the minimum and maximum values.

This is a screenshot of the extraction of data required for the football field chart:

Summary of Valuation Results - Share Price for Wazobia Global Ltd.				
Method	**EV/Sales**	**EV/EBITDA**	**P/E**	**DCF**
DCF	-	-	-	117.2
Trading Comparatives	62.2	46.8	43.3	-
Transaction Comparatives	75.2	46.2	35.4	-
Lowest and Highest Valuations				
Method	**Lowest (N)**	**Highest (N)**	**Difference**	
DCF	117.2	117.2	0.0	
EV/Sales	=MIN(C64:C65)		13.0	
EV/EBITDA	46.2	46.8	0.6	
P/E	35.4	43.3	7.9	
P/E	35.4	43.3	7.9	

Let's go through the following steps:

1. Using the MIN and MAX functions, you extract the lowest and highest share price values that are calculated using each of the listed methods—DCF, EV/Sales, EV/EBITDA, and P/E.

2. Go to **Insert** | **Chart** | **2-D Bar**, and choose the second option, as shown here:

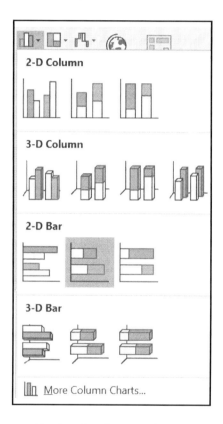

3. A blank chart appears. Resize the chart and move it to just below your table:

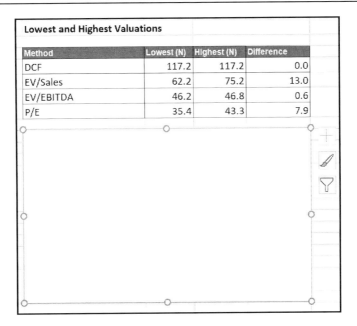

Lowest and Highest Valuations			
Method	Lowest (N)	Highest (N)	Difference
DCF	117.2	117.2	0.0
EV/Sales	62.2	75.2	13.0
EV/EBITDA	46.2	46.8	0.6
P/E	35.4	43.3	7.9

4. Go to the **Chart Tools | Design** ribbon, then click on **Select Data**:

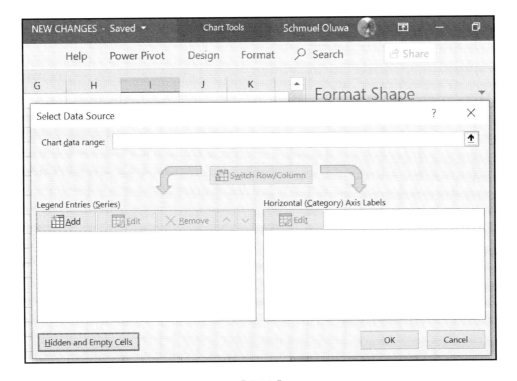

5. In the **Select Data Source** dialog box, you will add the data series. We have three data series, Lowest, Highest, and Difference, but for the moment, we will only use the Lowest and Difference series. In the **Legend Entries (Series)** section, click on **Add**, then select the range of values under the lowest column **C70** to **C73**:

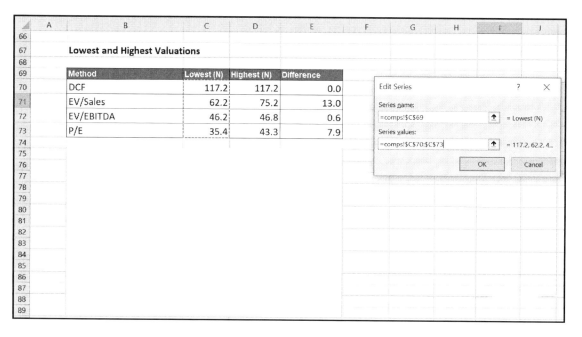

6. Repeat the procedure and add the second data series **E70** to **E73**:

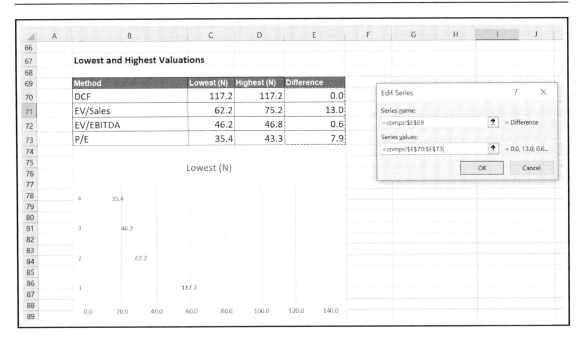

7. Right-click any of the data points of the `Lowest` series and then click on **Format Series**. In the **Format Data Labels** dialog box, click on the **Fill** icon and select **No fill**:

8. Now select the `Method` section as the horizontal axis, **B70** to **B73**:

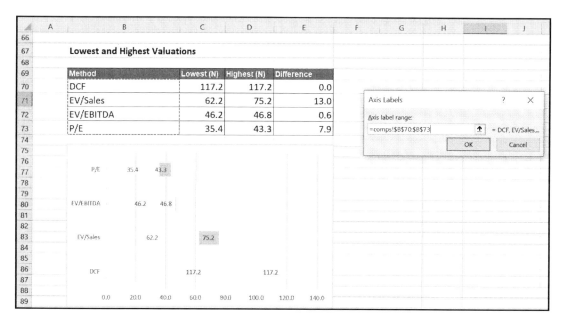

9. If the data labels are not displayed at the data points, follow this and the next step to display them. Click on any point of the `Lowest` series. Then go to **Chart Tools | Design| Add Chart Element| Data Labels | Inside Base**:

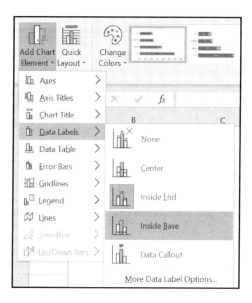

10. For the data labels of the `Difference` series, we want to display the values for the `Maximum` series. Go to **Chart Tools | Design | Add Chart Element | Data Labels | Inside End**. Right-click on any one of these data points; then, in the **Format Data Labels** dialog box, under **Label Options**, check **Value From Cells**, click on **Select Range...**, and select cells **D70** to **D73**:

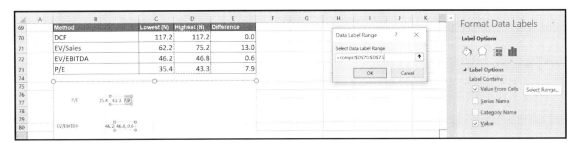

11. The maximum values are displayed against the `Difference` points. Under **Label Options| Label Contains**, uncheck the **Value** box.

12. In this way, we have displayed on the chart the minimum and maximum values obtained for each of the methods used—`DCF`, `EV/Sales`, `EV/EBITDA`, and `P/E`:

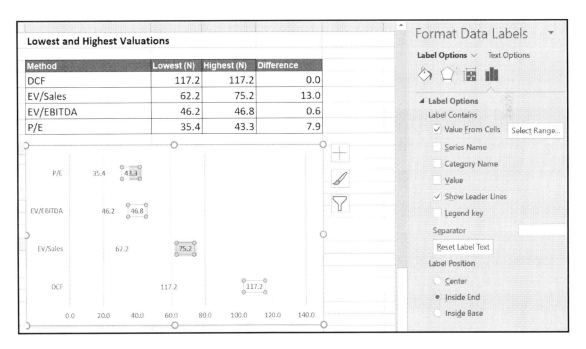

13. Finally, go to the **Chart Tools** | **Design** ribbon, then click on **Add Chart Element** | **Chart Title** | **Above Chart**. Type in the chart title in the text box that appears at the top of the chart:

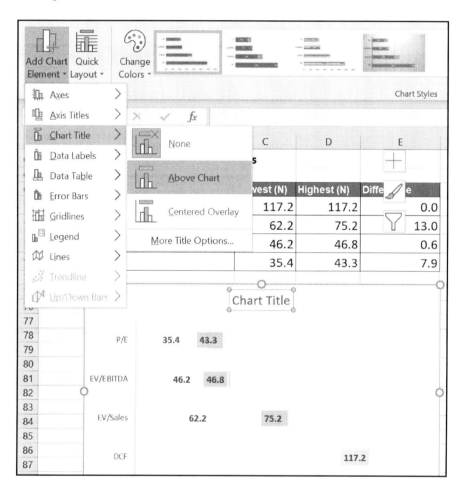

14. Click on the DCF `Lowest` series point, then click again to deselect the other points, leaving only the DCF point selected, then delete. We do this because there is only one value for the DCF method. We now have the completed football field chart:

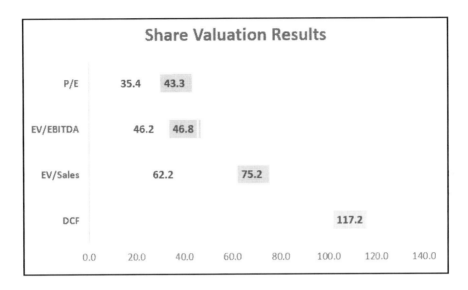

From the results, we can draw the following conclusions:

- The shares of Wazobia Global Ltd. should be quoted as being between naira **35.4** and naira **117.2**.
- If the price falls below naira **35.4**, the shares are undervalued, and you should buy. Since the shares are undervalued, there is every likelihood that the price will go up, and you could then sell at a profit.
- If the price goes above naira **117.2**, the shares are overvalued and there is every likelihood that the price will drop. Do not buy, and if you bought shares earlier at a lower price, now is the time to sell them at a profit before the price drops back down.

Summary

In this chapter, we have looked at three different methods of valuation:

- Absolute valuation using the discounted cash flow method
- Relative valuation using trading comparatives
- Relative valuation using transaction comparatives

We have learned that the DCF method is widely accepted as the most accurate, but because of its simplicity and ease of application, relative valuation is also popular among investment analysts. We have seen that there is no one correct answer; rather, we arrive at a range of results that give us a range within which the share price should fall. We have also learned how to create a football field chart to display our results and have learned how to interpret them in a meaningful way.

In the next chapter, *Model Testing for Reasonableness and Accuracy*, we will test our model to see how it responds to changes in certain key variables. We will also learn how to plot our findings in a torpedo chart. We will consider what steps we should take in the course of our modeling to ensure that errors are kept to a minimum. Nevertheless, since errors are inevitable, we will also look at troubleshooting procedures.

10
Model Testing for Reasonableness and Accuracy

Preparing a financial model involves a lot of assumptions and subjective decisions. In order to reduce the effects of this subjectivity as much as possible, you will need to adopt certain procedures, some of which we have already mentioned, and carry out certain tests designed to highlight the most volatile assumptions and pay direct attention to those inputs to which the model is most sensitive.

In this chapter, we will cover the following topics:

- Incorporating built-in tests and procedures
- Troubleshooting
- Understanding sensitivity analysis
- Using direct and indirect methods
- Understanding scenario analysis
- Creating a simple Monte Carlo simulation model

Incorporating built-in tests and procedures

A financial model, by its very nature, is full of formulas and calculations. Although most of them are simple, their volume and repetitiveness create an exposure to errors that could give the most accomplished modeler nightmares when trying to track them down.

The following are some of the procedures to adopt in your model in order to reduce this exposure:

- **Hardcoded cells**: These should be distinguished by using a blue font. The following screenshot shows hardcoded cells in a blue font, to distinguish them from calculated cells, which are in the standard black font:

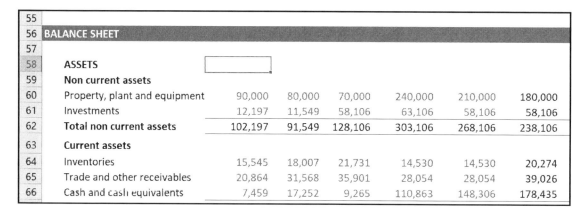

If a model has to be modified, it is these hardcoded cells that will need to be adjusted to effect the required change. Using the blue font reduces the time it will take to navigate to the cells that need to be modified.

- **Balance check**: Creating a balance check for the balance sheet ensures that you are able to confirm that it is in balance, and quickly identify any action that causes it to go out of balance. The balance check should be conspicuous and differentiate clearly between in-balance and out-of-balance conditions.

- For the balance sheet to be in balance, **Total assets less current liabilities** must equal **Total equity and non-current liabilities**. If there is a rounding off difference that is not displayed, this would still cause an out-of-balance alert. This is why you should use the ROUND function to make sure Excel ignores the decimal figures when comparing the two totals.

The following screenshot shows an example of a balance check:

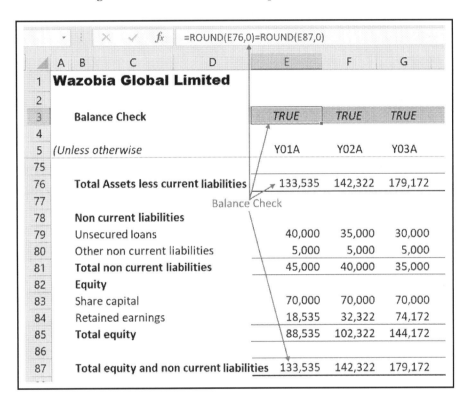

- **Cash and cash equivalents**: Cash and cash equivalents on the balance sheet should be the same as the closing cash balance for the corresponding year in the cash flow statement. This gives some assurance that, up to that point, the model is mathematically accurate.

- **Enter values only once**: If there is a need to enter a value again, simply refer to the cell containing the original entry of that value. This reduces the exposure to error and ensures that if that value has to be modified, you only need to adjust the original entry, and all other occurrences will be updated accordingly.
- **Use one formula per row**: Make use of Excel's referencing framework, which is explained in `Chapter 4`, *Applying the Referencing Framework In Excel*, to enter a formula once, and fill in the same formula along the row, to the right, for the rest of the years. If done properly, this will greatly reduce the modeling time and reduce the incidence of errors.

Troubleshooting

In the event that there is an error, there are certain steps you can take to quickly eliminate several possibilities:

- **Precedents**: Precedents are those cells that have been referred to in arriving at the value in a particular cell
- **Dependents**: Dependents are those cells that have included the cell in focus in their formula

The following screenshot will be used to explain this further:

	A	B	C	D	J	K	L
1							
2		(Unless otherwise specified, all financials are in N '000)			Y06F	Y07F	Y08F
3							
4		**DCF Valuation using FCFF**					
6		EBIT			55,658	66,822	78,542
7		Tax Rate (%)		30.0%			
8		EBIT*(1-t)			38,961	=K6*(1-$D$7)	
9		Add: Depreciation			30,000	30,000	30,000
10		Change in Working Capital			(15,107)	12,028	(15,245)
11		Less: Capex and increase in WIP			-	-	-
12		**Free Cashflow to the Firm (FCFF)**			53,854	88,803	69,734

From the preceding screenshot, let's look at cell **K8**. The formula in that cell is
=K6*(1-$D$7), so cells **K6** and **D7** are the precedents of cell **K8**. On the other
hand, cell **K8** is a dependent of both cells **K6** and **D7**.

On the **Formula** ribbon, in the **Formula Auditing** group, selecting **Trace
Precedents** or **Trace Dependents** reveals thin blue arrows linking a cell to either
its precedents or its dependents, accordingly.

The following screenshot shows us how we can use Excel to visualize dependents
and precedents:

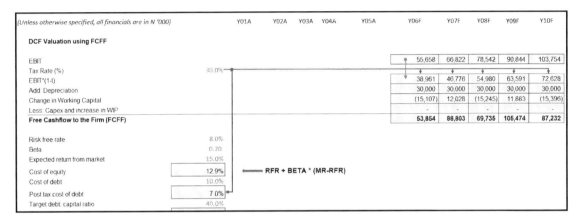

(Unless otherwise specified, all financials are in N '000)		Y01A	Y02A	Y03A	Y04A	Y05A	Y06F	Y07F	Y08F	Y09F	Y10F
DCF Valuation using FCFF											
EBIT							55,658	66,822	78,542	90,844	103,754
Tax Rate (%)	30.0%										
EBIT*(1-t)							38,961	46,776	54,980	63,591	72,628
Add: Depreciation							30,000	30,000	30,000	30,000	30,000
Change in Working Capital							(15,107)	12,028	(15,245)	11,883	(15,396)
Less: Capex and increase in WIP							-	-	-	-	-
Free Cashflow to the Firm (FCFF)							**53,854**	**88,803**	**69,735**	**105,474**	**87,232**
Risk free rate	8.0%										
Beta	0.70										
Expected return from market	15.0%										
Cost of equity	12.9%	RFR + BETA * (MR-RFR)									
Cost of debt	10.0%										
Post tax cost of debt	7.0%										
Target debt: capital ratio	40.0%										

We can see that cell **D7** has several dependents. However, since it is a hardcoded entry, it has no precedents. If any cell has an issue, tracing precedents and/or dependents can reveal erroneous referencing that may have caused the anomaly.

- **Show formulas**: There is a useful keyboard shortcut, *Ctrl + `*, that allows you to toggle between displaying the formulas in all relevant cells in a worksheet or leaving them as values. Pressing *Ctrl + `* once displays all of the formulas in the worksheet, as shown in the following screenshot:

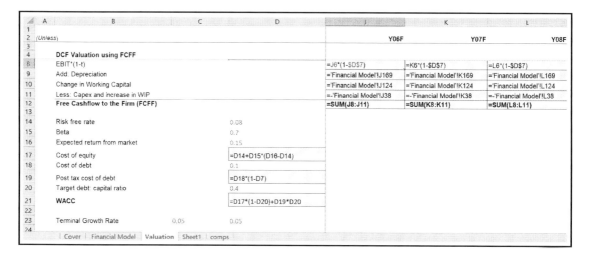

	A	B	C	D		J	K	L
1								
2	*(Unless)*					Y06F	Y07F	Y08F
3								
4		**DCF Valuation using FCFF**						
8		EBIT*(1-t)				=J6*(1-$D$7)	=K6*(1-$D$7)	=L6*(1-$D$7)
9		Add: Depreciation				='Financial Model'!J169	='Financial Model'!K169	='Financial Model'!L169
10		Change in Working Capital				='Financial Model'!J124	='Financial Model'!K124	='Financial Model'!L124
11		Less: Capex and increase in WIP				=-'Financial Model'!J38	=-'Financial Model'!K38	=-'Financial Model'!L38
12		**Free Cashflow to the Firm (FCFF)**				=SUM(J8:J11)	=SUM(K8:K11)	=SUM(L8:L11)
13								
14		Risk free rate		0.08				
15		Beta		0.7				
16		Expected return from market		0.15				
17		Cost of equity		=D14+D15*(D16-D14)				
18		Cost of debt		0.1				
19		Post tax cost of debt		=D18*(1-D7)				
20		Target debt: capital ratio		0.4				
21		**WACC**		=D17*(1-D20)+D19*D20				
22								
23		Terminal Growth Rate	0.05	0.05				
24								

| Cover | Financial Model | Valuation | Sheet1 | comps |

Pressing *Ctrl+`* again returns the display to values, as shown in the following screenshot:

	A	B	C	D	J	K	L
1							
2	*(Unless otherwise specified, all financials are in N '000)*				**Y06F**	**Y07F**	**Y08F**
3							
4		**DCF Valuation using FCFF**					
8		EBIT*(1-t)			38,961	46,776	54,980
9		Add: Depreciation			30,000	30,000	30,000
10		Change in Working Capital			(15,107)	12,028	(15,245)
11		Less: Capex and increase in WIP			-	-	-
12		**Free Cashflow to the Firm (FCFF)**			**53,854**	**88,803**	**69,734**
13							
14		Risk free rate		8.0%			
15		Beta		0.70			
16		Expected return from market		15.0%			
17		Cost of equity		12.9%			
18		Cost of debt		10.0%			
19		Post tax cost of debt		7.0%			
20		Target debt: capital ratio		40.0%			
21		**WACC**		10.5% t * wt			
22							
23		Terminal Growth Ra	5.0%	5.0%			

This is useful in that it allows you to quickly browse through the formulas in a worksheet and spot any obvious errors.

- **Evaluate formula**: There is an **order of operations** that states the order in which operands (+, -, x, \, and ^) will be performed by Excel—brackets, then exponents, then multiplication, division (whichever is first, from left to right), and then addition and subtraction (whichever is first, from left to right). When you have to write complex formulas with several operands, the following order of operations helps to ensure that the formula executes correctly. Inevitably, there will be times when you arrange a formula incorrectly and get the order wrong, resulting in an erroneous answer.

The **Evaluate Formula** feature walks you, step by step, through the stages followed by Excel in executing a formula and arriving at the answer displayed. For example, the formula to calculate the terminal value is as follows:

$$\text{FINAL YEAR FCFF} \times \frac{(1 + \text{TGR})}{(\text{WACC-TGR})}$$

This formula, when entered into an Excel cell, becomes the following:

```
=N12*(1+D23)/(D21-D23)
```

With the terminal value cell selected, go to **Evaluate Formula** (**Formula** ribbon>**Formula Editing** group>**Evaluate Formula**). The **Evaluate Formula** dialog box is launched, as demonstrated in the following screenshot:

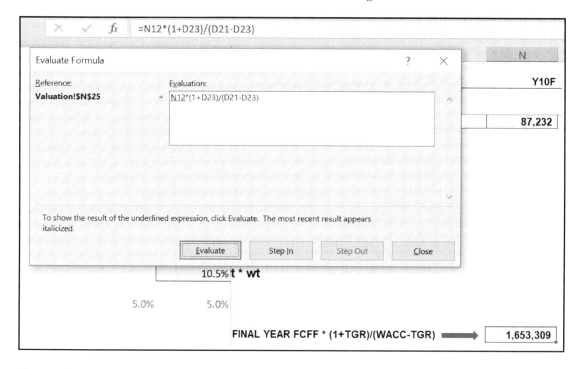

The **Evaluate Formula** dialog box displays the cell with the formula being evaluated (in this case, N25), the formula itself, which is reproduced in the **Evaluation** box, and four buttons at the bottom of the dialog box; namely, **Evaluate**, **Step In**, **Step Out**, and **Close**. In the **Evaluation** box, the next item to be evaluated is underlined. This could be an operation (+, -, x, \, ^), converting a cell reference to the value in that cell, or removing brackets from a part of the equation.

Excel, by default, will execute a formula from left to right until it gets to a decision point where there is an option to execute an operand of higher rank that will result in a different answer. Excel will then jump to that higher-ranked operand and execute it first before returning to the lower-ranked operand and continue from left to right.

In the formula in **N25**, the first step is for Excel to convert the first reference, **N12**, and FCFF, to the value in that cell. Accordingly, in the preceding screenshot, the reference **N12** is underlined. The following screenshots take us, step by step, through the execution of the formula:

Evaluation:

= 87231.7207445792*(1+D23)/(D21-D23)

The reference **N12** is now replaced by its value. Notice how Excel does not show the abbreviated amount, 87,232, which is as a result of rounding off through formatting, but the full figure to 10 decimal places.

The next operand in sequence should be multiplication. However, brackets are ranked higher than multiplication and will therefore take precedence. The contents within the brackets will thus be fully executed before Excel returns to the default left-to-right sequence.

In the following screenshot, the reference D23 within the first set of brackets is now underlined, signifying that it will be executed next:

Evaluation:

= 87231.7207445792*(1+0.05)/(D21-D23)

The reference D23 is now replaced by its value, 0.05 (5%), and the line now sits under the contents of the first set of brackets, signifying that the addition, even though it is of lower rank, will be executed next to give (1.05):

Evaluation:

= 87231.7207445792*(1.05)/(D21-D23)

In the following screenshot, the brackets around 1.05 are removed, and the line now returns to the normal sequence and sits under the multiplication:

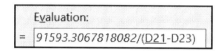

The following screenshot shows the result of the multiplication:

Evaluation:

= 91593.3067818082/(D21-D23)

The cell reference, D21, will then be converted to its value:

Evaluation:

= 91593.3067818082/(0.1054-D23)

Now, D23 will be replaced by its value, as displayed in the cell:

Evaluation:

= 91593.3067818082/(0.1054-0.05)

In the following two screenshots, the result of the subtraction is displayed and then the brackets are removed. First of all, the subtraction is evaluated:

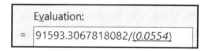

Next, the brackets are removed, introducing the figure within them to the formula:

Evaluation:

= 91593.3067818082/0.0554

Then, the final operand, division, is executed to give the result of the formula, as displayed in the following screenshot:

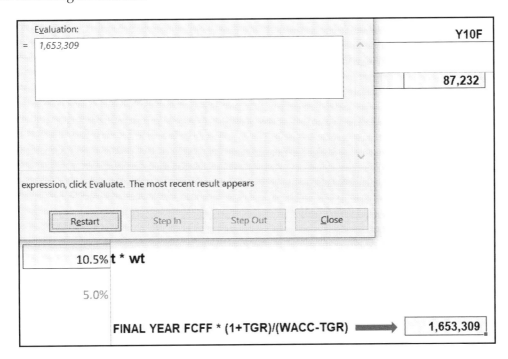

 You should note that if, at any stage, an error is detected within the formula, you can click on **Step In** to pause the evaluation, step into the formula, effect the correction, and then click **Step Out** to resume the evaluation.

Understanding sensitivity analysis

In Chapter 9, *Valuation*, we computed a value for equity share price. As a result of the uncertainty inherent in your model, you should take some steps to mitigate this. One way is to run some tests to see how the share price behaves when you change some of the inputs and drivers utilized in arriving at that value.

This process is called **sensitivity analysis**. Apart from the volatility of your target value, it also indicates which inputs or drivers have the greatest effect on the target value. You will need to identify two inputs or drivers that appear to hold prominence in your model.

We have already mentioned that turnover is the most prominent figure in the income statement. So, we can use the revenue growth driver as one of the items to sensitize. Another item of prominence is the terminal value.

We have seen in `Chapter 9`, *Valuation*, how much of an impact this has on your share price valuation. You could use the terminal growth rate, which is a variable used in arriving at terminal value, as the second item to sensitize. The idea is to vary these inputs, see what effect it has on your share price, and plot the results.

Using direct and indirect methods

There are two methods in sensitivity analysis: the direct and indirect methods. Both methods make use of data tables that can be found under **What If** in the **Forecast** group on the **Data** ribbon in Excel. The following is a screenshot of the location of the **Data Table...** option:

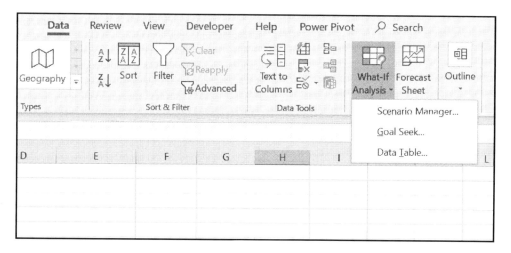

In order to make use of the data table, you must structure your data in a particular way. The following screenshot shows the layout for a data table:

Share Price (NAIRA)	117.2				
			TERMINAL GROWTH RATE		
		117.2	0.0%		
	REVENUE GROWTH	0.0%			
	(CAGR)	2.5%			

The cell in the top-left corner of the table layout must be related to the target value share price, whose behavior we wish to observe. That specific position is essential for the data table function to work. However, since it will not be used for anything else, it is shown here in a white font color, making it invisible to the naked eye, so as not to cause any distraction.

The row input values are entered across the top row of the table. We have selected **TERMINAL GROWTH RATE** for the row input, with values from 3% and 1% increments up to 7%. The column input is **REVENUE GROWTH (CAGR)** and is entered down the far-left column of the table, with values from 0% and 2.5% increments up to 9.5%.

However, the 5% entry is changed to 4.5% to agree with the actual historical CAGR used as the turnover growth driver. In preparation for the data table function, select the entire table from the cell with the target value at the top left, excluding the input/driver values. Then, select **Data Table...** from the **What If** menu, of the forecast group on the **Data** ribbon. This launches the **Data Table** dialog box, as shown in the following screenshot:

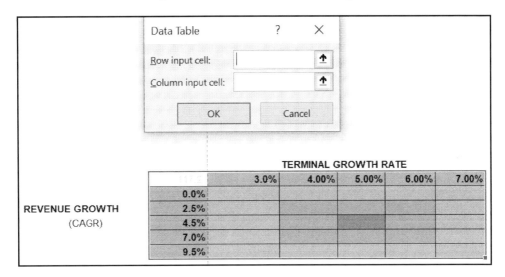

The **Data Table** dialog box has two inputs, **Row input cell** and **Column input cell**.

The direct method

In this method, the row and column input cells are linked directly to the model via the cells in which they appear in the model. In this case, the **Row input cell** is the **TERMINAL GROWTH RATE** cell in the **Valuation** section that is linked to your model; cell **D265**. The **Column input cell** is the turnover growth driver for Y06F, in the **Assumptions** section, that is linked to your model, cell **J11**.

The following screenshot is an illustration of the **Row input cell**:

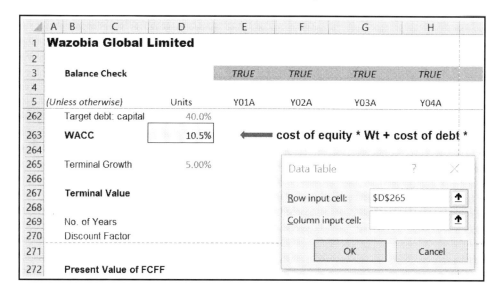

The following screenshot is an illustration of the **Column input cell**:

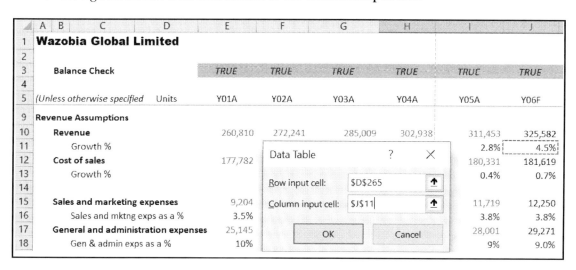

When you press **OK**, the data table is filled with the results generated from substituting the terminal growth rate and turnover growth driver in your model, with the alternative values in the data table row and column headers. The following is a screenshot of the completed data table:

		TERMINAL GROWTH RATE				
	117.2	3.0%	4.00%	5.00%	6.00%	7.00%
REVENUE GROWTH (CAGR)	0.0%	80.2	91.1	105.9	127.3	160.7
	2.5%	85.2	96.6	112.1	134.5	169.5
	4.5%	89.1	101.0	117.1	140.3	176.6
	7.0%	94.1	106.4	123.3	147.5	185.4
	9.5%	99.0	111.9	129.4	154.7	194.3

You can test the accuracy of your data table by looking at the share value at a 5% terminal growth rate and a 4.5% turnover growth driver.

Your table has been arranged so that this value is right in the middle of the table, in the cell with the darker green fill. It shows `117.1`, compared to your valuation result of `117.2`. This gives you confidence that your data table is set up right and calculating correctly.

From the table, we see that the lowest share price is N`80.2` at 3% terminal growth rate and 0% revenue growth, and the highest share price is N`194.3`, obtained with a terminal growth rate at 7% and revenue growth at 9.5%.

The indirect method

This method links the table to formulas that include the variables or drivers we have selected. To do this, we first set up data tables, as shown in the following screenshot:

Turnover Growth +/-2.5%	
Change	Share Price (N)
0.0%	117.2
-2.5%	
2.5%	

Cost of Sales +/-2.5%	
Change	Share Price (N)
0.0%	117.2
-2.5%	
2.5%	

Terminal Growth Rate +/-1%	
Change	Share Price (N)
0.0%	117.2
-1.0%	
1.0%	

All three inputs have a change base value of 0.0%, which will be added to formulas that include the inputs we have selected. Then, we also add two additional values of -2.5% and 2.5% for turnover growth and cost of sales, and -1.0% and 1.0 for terminal growth rate. The change values signify the range over which we will be testing the sensitivity of our model with data tables using the indirect method.

You then edit the relevant formulas to link the data tables to the model by adding the 0.0% cells. For example, the turnover for Y06F, the first year of forecasts, is arrived at by applying the turnover growth driver to the turnover of the previous year, Y05A, as seen in the following formula:

$$\text{Last year's turnover} \times (1 + \text{turnover growth driver})$$
$$= I10 \times (1 + J11)$$

You will edit the formula to add the base value for the turnover growth driver from your data table, 0.0%, in cell **C295**, as follows:

```
=I10*(1+J11+C295)
```

You should then copy the formula across the other forecast years. In this way, you have linked the data table to your model without changing its result:

	A	B	C	D	H	I	J
							f_x =I12*(1+J13+$F$295)
2							
3		**Balance Check**			*TRUE*	*TRUE*	*TRUE*
4							
5		*(Unless otherwise specified, all financial*		Units	Y04A	Y05A	Y06F
6							
7		ASSUMPTIONS					
8							
9		**Revenue Assumptions**					
10		Revenue			302,938	311,453	325,582
11		Growth %			6.3%	2.8%	4.5%
12		**Cost of sales**			179,690	180,331	=I12*(1+J13+$F$295)
13		Growth %			0.4%	0.4%	0.7%

In the same way, link the `Cost of Sales` data table to the formula in cell **J12**:

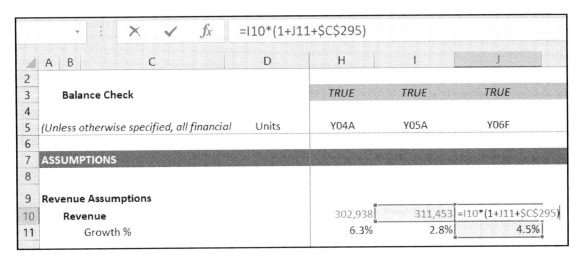

Then, link the terminal growth rate data table to the formula in cell **N267**.

Note that the terminal growth rate appears twice in this formula, so the modification has to be implemented in relation to each occurrence of the input.

The following screenshot shows how you link the terminal growth rate data table to your model:

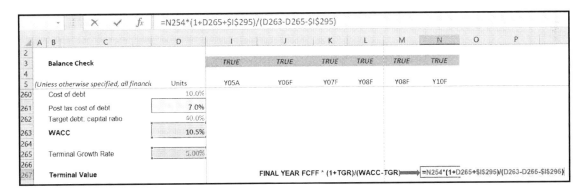

You can now go back and populate your data table with the **What-If Analysis, Data Table** feature. First, select the entire turnover growth table:

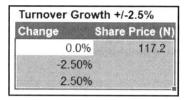

Go to **Data Table** under **Data>What-If Analysis**, or use the keyboard shortcut *Alt + A + W + T*, to bring up the **Data Table** dialog box. The following is a screenshot of the **Data Table** dialog box:

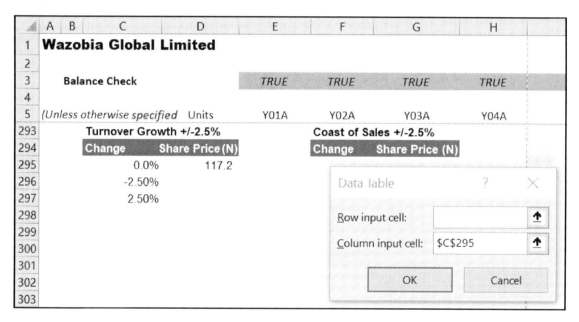

Leave the **Row input cell** blank and select the cell with 0.0% as the **Column input cell**. When you click **OK**, the data table will be populated with calculated values for the share price at a turnover growth rate of 2.5% below the original rate, and 2.5% above the original rate.

The following screenshot shows the populated `Turnover Growth Rate` data table:

Turnover Growth +/-2.5%	
Change	**Share Price (N)**
0.0%	117.2
-2.5%	84.4
2.5%	153.0

Repeat the same for the `Cost of Sales` and `Terminal Growth Rate` data tables. This is a screenshot of the complete data tables using the indirect method:

Turnover Growth +/-2.5%		Cost of Sales +/-2.5%		Terminal Growth Rate +/-1%	
Change	**Share Price (N)**	**Change**	**Share Price (N)**	**Change**	**Share Price (N)**
0.0%	117.2	0.0%	117.2	0.0%	117.2
-2.5%	84.4	-2.5%	138.3	-1.0%	101.0
2.5%	153.0	2.5%	93.9	1.0%	140.4

Checking your data table again, you will notice that it is 2.5% above the base turnover growth of 4.5%; in other words, 7.0%.

At 7% turnover growth and a 5% terminal growth rate, using the direct method, we get a share price of N123.3, which is in agreement with the value in our indirect method database for turnover growth. At a 4% terminal growth rate and a 4.5% turnover growth rate, using the direct method, we get a share price of N101.0, which is in agreement with the value in our indirect method database for the terminal growth rate.

As they stand, the indirect method data tables are difficult to understand, so you will need to go a step further and prepare a **tornado chart**. A tornado chart is an effective way of showing the impact of changes in a number of inputs and drivers in one place. You will start off by preparing a table with the information required for the chart, from the indirect method data tables.

The first step is to calculate the percentage change in share price from the base value to the value at the negative change. We are not interested in whether the change is negative or positive, and only require the absolute change. So, we will use the following formula:

$$ABS((\text{new share price - base share price})/\text{base share price})\%$$

A percentage change in share price, accompanied by a change in input or driver, is displayed in the following screenshot:

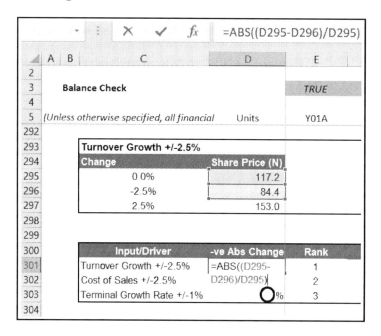

Repeat this formula for the cost of sales and terminal growth rate. Now, rank the smallest percentage change first using the following formula:

```
=SMALL(% change, rank number)
```

Copy the formula down the next two rows so that the rank number will change from 1 to 2, and then to 3. This will result in the percentage being ranked smallest to largest, as seen in the following screenshot:

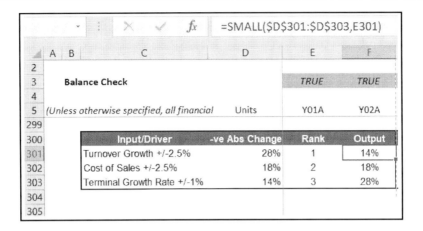

Using the `INDEX` and `MATCH` functions (refer to `Chapter 3`, *Formulas and Functions*), enter the appropriate input and driver name beside the ranked output (absolute change). These will serve as our horizontal axis labels.

The following is a screenshot of the `INDEX` and `MATCH` formulas:

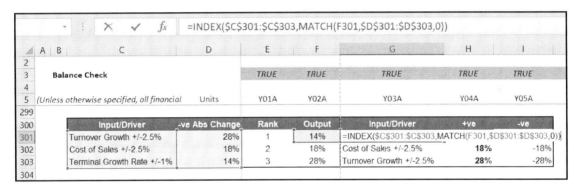

Bring the output to the right of the labels and form two series, one positive and the other negative, of the same figures. The following screenshot shows the complete table:

Input/Driver	-ve Abs Change	Rank	Output	Input/Driver	+ve	-ve
Turnover Growth +/-2.5%	28%	1	14%	Terminal Growth Rate +/-1%	14%	-14%
Cost of Sales +/-2.5%	18%	2	18%	Cost of Sales +/-2.5%	18%	-18%
Terminal Growth Rate +/-1%	14%	3	28%	Turnover Growth +/-2.5%	28%	-28%

Now, create a chart by going to **Insert>Column or bar chart**, and then select **2-D stacked bar chart**. A blank chart will be placed on your worksheet. From the context-sensitive chart design menu, click on **Select Data** and the **Select Data Source** dialog box opens up, as follows:

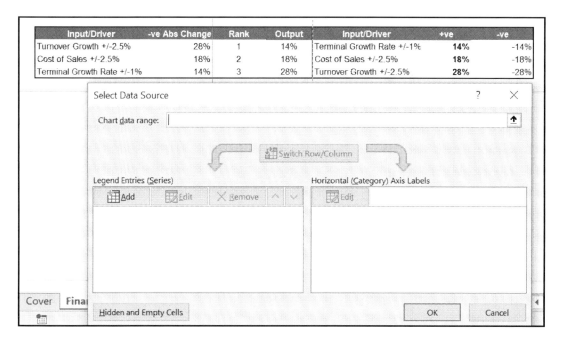

Now, add the two series, one after the other, by selecting **Add** under **Legend Entries (Series)**. The **Edit Series** dialog box opens up. Select the column of positive output as the first series. Selection of the first data series is shown in the following screenshot:

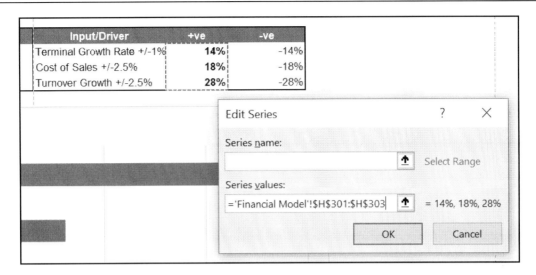

Input/Driver	+ve	-ve
Terminal Growth Rate +/-1%	14%	-14%
Cost of Sales +/-2.5%	18%	-18%
Turnover Growth +/-2.5%	28%	-28%

Edit Series

Series name:

Series values:
='Financial Model'!$H$301:$H$303   = 14%, 18%, 28%

OK   Cancel

Repeat the procedure to add the second series. Selection of the second data series is shown in the following screenshot:

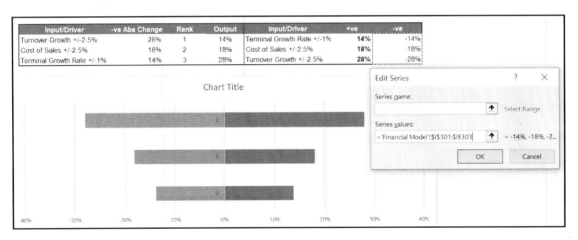

Now, select the horizontal axis labels. Click **Edit**, and then select the column with the input and driver names. The following screenshot shows editing of the horizontal axis labels:

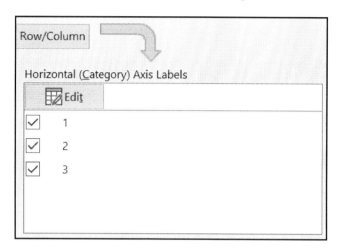

The following screenshot shows an alternative way to edit horizontal axis labels:

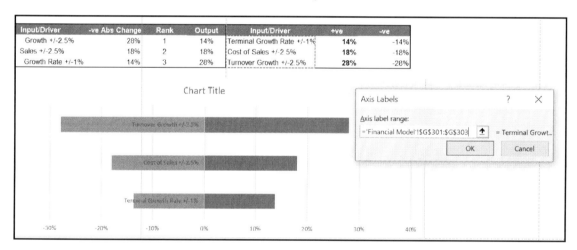

The labels will appear against the horizontal axis, within the negative series data:

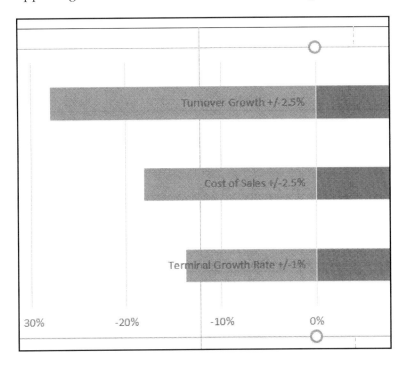

Double-click on the horizontal axis to launch the **Format Axis** dialog box, as shown in the following screenshot:

 Remember that your chart is a stacked bar chart and is therefore flipped on its side so that the horizontal axis is actually vertical.

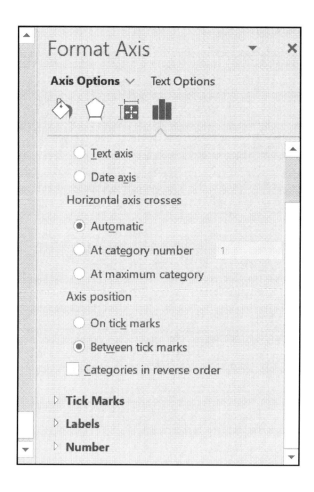

Scroll down to reveal the **Labels** option and click on it. Change the label position to Low:

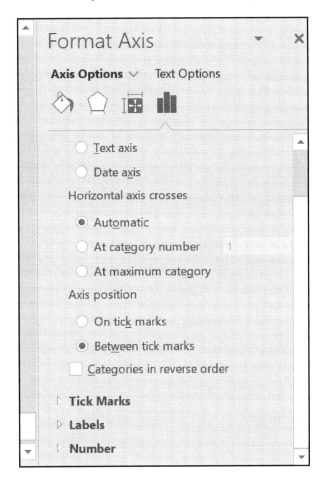

This results in the following output:

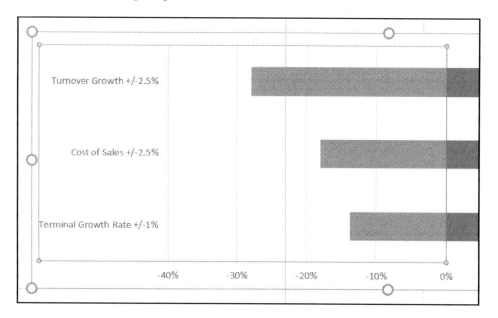

Now, click on the colored series one after the other and change the color to a more suitable one:

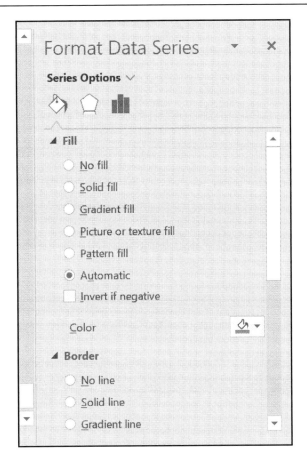

Add a chart title and edit it to give it appropriate prominence:

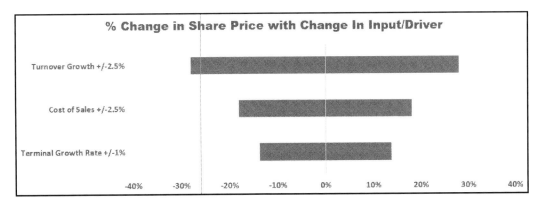

The chart clearly shows that changing the turnover growth driver has the most significant effect on the share price, followed by the cost of sales and, finally, the terminal growth rate.

Understanding scenario analysis

In sensitivity analysis, we selected a few inputs or drivers and changed them, while keeping all other variables the same. This showed us the isolated effect that each of the selected inputs has on share price. However, in practice, this is rarely the case. Variables do not change in isolation. What you generally have is a number of variables changing as a result of a certain set of circumstances, or a scenario. Scenario analysis usually looks at two or three sets of circumstances, most likely, worst-case and best-case scenarios.

For each scenario, you would assume alternative values for selected variables. In selecting the variables, you would concentrate on those inputs or drivers that are the most subjective. Scenario analysis involves substituting all the selected variables for a given scenario in your model and examining the effect this has on the share price. We will look at optimistic, base, and pessimistic scenarios. We will also select **Turnover CAGR**, **TGR**, and **WACC**, as these variables have a significant effect on share price.

Set up your table as shown in the following screenshot, with appropriate values to reflect optimistic and pessimistic scenarios, respectively. The base case will reflect the calculated values from our DCF valuation. The following screenshot shows the scenario table:

	Turnover CAGR	TGR	WACC
Optimistic	6.0%	5.5%	9.0%
Base Case	4.5%	5.0%	10.5%
Pessimistic	3.0%	4.5%	12.0%

SHARE PRICE

We now need to set up a selection box that will allow us to select a scenario and link the scenario to the values we have chosen for each scenario. We will be using a combo box for this, along with the OFFSET function. This combo box can be found under **Insert** in the **Controls** group in Excel on the **Developer** tab. If the **Developer** tab is not displayed, go to **File>Options>Customize the Ribbon**. Under **Main Tabs**, check the box beside **Developer**.

The following screenshot shows the location of **Combo Box** on the **Developer** tab:

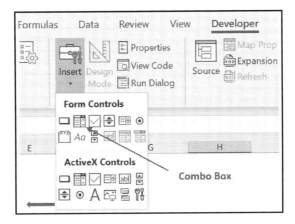

Position the **Combo Box** beside the reference box, right-click on the combo box, and select **Format Control**. The **Format Object** dialog box is launched, as shown in the following screenshot:

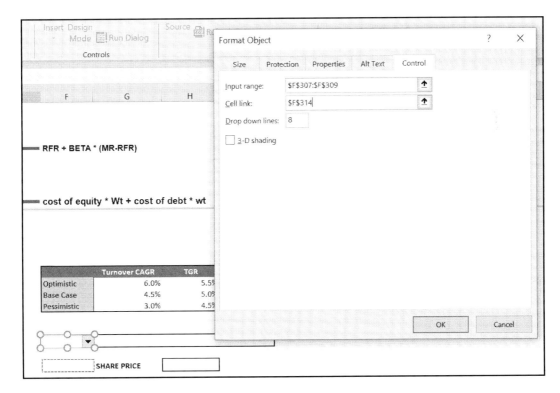

For the **Input range**, select the cells with the scenario labels. **Cell link** can be any blank cell. Select the cell to the left of the SHARE PRICE label. The following screenshot shows the **Format Object** dialog box for the **Combo Box**:

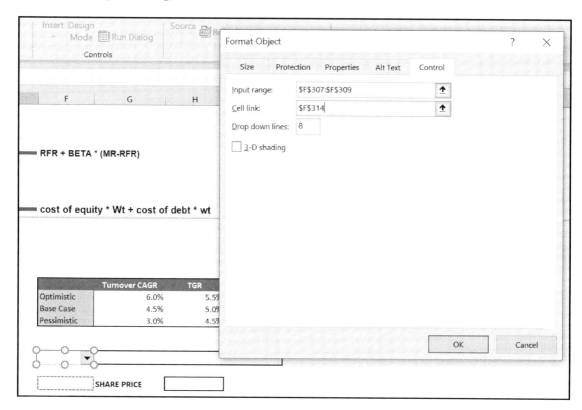

Click on the arrow to the right of the combo box. A drop-down list is revealed with the scenario names. The following screenshot is the drop-down list of **Combo Box** options:

	Turnover CAGR	TGR	WACC
Optimistic	6.0%	5.5%	9.0%
Base Case	4.5%	5.0%	10.5%
Pessimistic	3.0%	4.5%	12.0%

Optimistic
Base Case
Pessimistic

SHARE PRICE

As soon as you select any of the options, they will be displayed in the combo box, and a number will be displayed in the **Cell link** cell, corresponding to the position in the list of the options you have selected. We now need to reflect the values of the variables for the selected scenario in the reference bar. To do this, we will use the OFFSET function, along with the counter in the **Cell Unit**. The arguments of the OFFSET function are arranged to allow you to guide Excel to a specific cell from which to extract the contents.

The following screenshot shows the arguments of the OFFSET function:

This function allows you to select a reference variable. The next argument, rows, allows you to specify a number of rows to offset down from that reference point; cols allows you to specify a number of columns to offset across from that reference point; height and width will only be used when you want to specify a range rather than a single cell.

The following screenshot shows the number 2 in the **Cell link**. When **Base Case**, the second in the list of scenarios is selected:

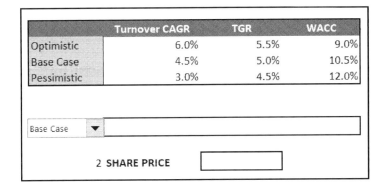

With the **Base Case** selected in the **Combo Box,** the number 2 is displayed in the **Cell link** (refer to the preceding screenshot. This corresponds to the position of **Base Case** in the drop-down list of the **Combo Box.** Next, select the cells in the reference box and then enter the OFFSET function.

Using our knowledge of Excel's referencing framework, we recognize that it is the same formula we are going to enter in the three cells in the reference box. We can therefore select the three cells, enter the formula once, and then press *Ctrl + Enter* to finish and populate all three cells at once. The following screenshot shows the values while entering the OFFSET formula parameters:

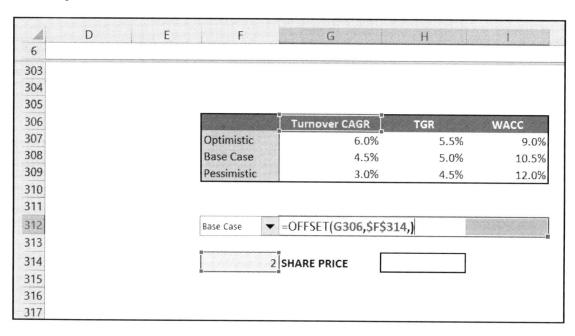

Make the reference cell **G306**, the Turnover CAGR heading. When the reference copies to the right, we want it to look at cell **H306**, the TGR heading, which is in the next column of the same row. Make the row cell $F$314 the **Cell link**. We are locking this cell reference, so that when the reference copies to the right, it will still look at the **Cell link**.

We then add a comma after the row argument to show that we have finished entering the parameters for that argument. However, since we are not entering any more arguments, we can close the brackets and then press *Ctrl +Enter* to finish and populate all three cells at once. Now, link the share price to the appropriate cell in the **Valuation** section of your model. We will also blank out the **Cell link** cell so that it does not cause a distraction. The following screenshot shows a scenario template with the share price linked and **Cell link** blanked out:

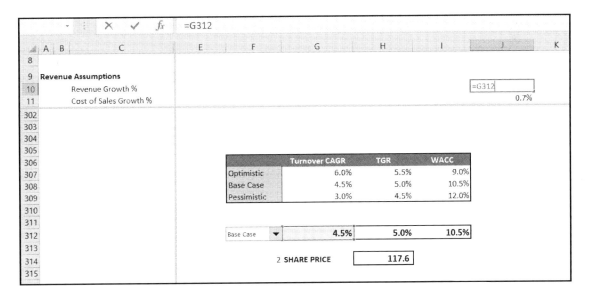

	Turnover CAGR	TGR	WACC
Optimistic	6.0%	5.5%	9.0%
Base Case	4.5%	5.0%	10.5%
Pessimistic	3.0%	4.5%	12.0%
Base Case ▼	4.5%	5.0%	10.5%
SHARE PRICE	117.6		

The next step is to link the cells in the reference box to the appropriate location in your model. First, relate the revenue growth CAGR cell from Assumptions, cell **I10**, to **G312** in the reference box. The following screenshot shows the scenario of linking the CAGR cell to the reference box:

Then, link TGR, cell **D247**, to cell **H312** in the reference box. The following screenshot shows how to link TGR to the reference box:

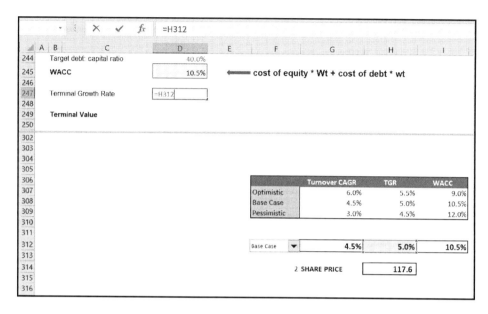

Then, link cell **D245**, WACC, to cell **H312** in the reference box. The following screenshot shows how to link WACC to the reference box:

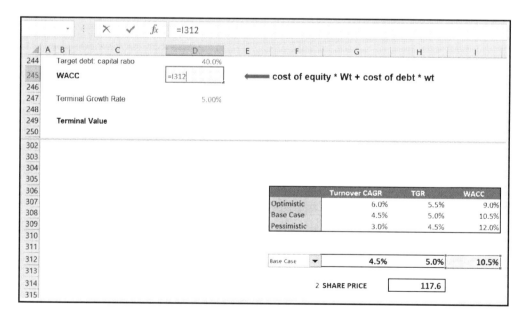

Finally, we use conditional formatting to highlight whichever scenario is currently selected. Go to **Conditional Formatting>New Rule...** on the **Home** ribbon. The following screenshot shows the **Conditional Formatting** option on the **Home** ribbon:

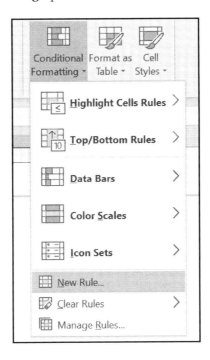

Select **New Rule...** to open up the **New Formatting Rule** dialog box:

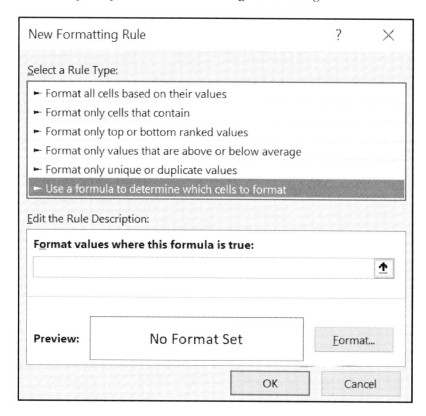

Now, select **Use a formula to determine which cells to format**.

We need to use this formula, instead of just selecting one of the preset options, because some of the cells with the condition we are going to specify are not the same cells to which the condition is to be applied. The following screenshot shows the **New Formatting Rule** dialog box:

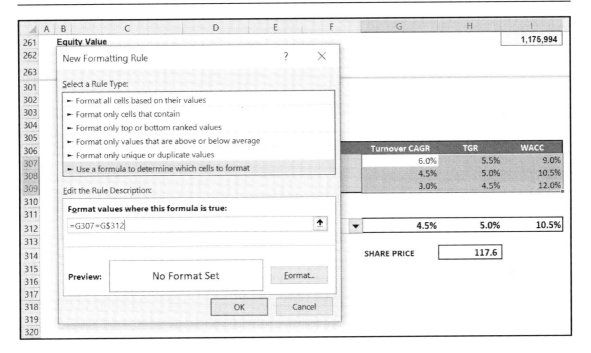

Once again, we will save time by using our knowledge of relative, absolute, and mixed referencing to enter the formula just once. The condition we will use is as follows: when any of the values in our scenario template equal the value in the same column on the reference box, then display the special format that we will specify.

We first highlight all the value cells in the scenario template, and then enter the formula as displayed in the preceding screenshot:

```
=G307=G$312
```

When that statement is true (it is currently false), that cell will display the special format we will specify. When the formula is copied to the right, `G307` becomes `H307`, and `G$312` becomes `H$312`. When the formula is copied down, `G307` becomes `G308`, and `G$312` stays as `G$312`. This ensures that the formula is always linked to the row of the reference box, row `312`.

Now that we are satisfied that the formula is correct, we press *Ctrl + Enter* to populate all the value cells in the scenario template with our formula. We can now specify the special format we want displayed when the condition is met. Select a bold and red style for the font. This screenshot shows how to specify a custom **Font** format:

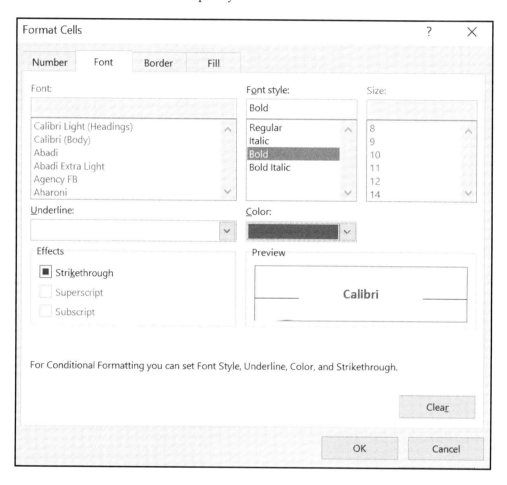

Now, we will select a better color fill. The following screenshot shows how to specify a custom **Fill** format:

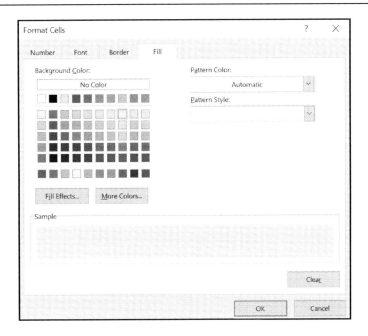

When you press **OK**, you are taken back to the **New Formatting Rule** dialog box, which now displays a sample of what the special format will look like. The following screenshot shows the **New Formatting Rule** dialog box with a sample of the custom format:

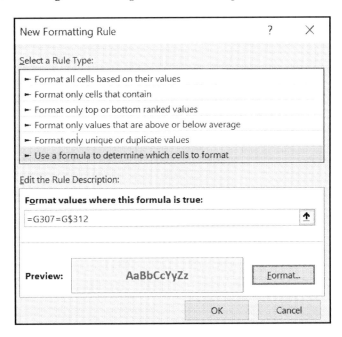

When you press **OK**, you are taken back to the worksheet and will observe that the values for **Base Case** display the conditional format. That is because that is the currently selected scenario in our **Combo Box**. Under the **Base Case** scenario, the share price is 117.6. The base case scenario with conditional formatting is as shown in the following screenshot:

	Turnover CAGR	TGR	WACC
Optimistic	6.0%	5.5%	9.0%
Base Case	4.5%	5.0%	10.5%
Pessimistic	3.0%	4.5%	12.0%
Base Case ▼	4.5%	5.0%	10.5%
SHARE PRICE	117.6		

In the **Combo Box**, select the Optimistic scenario. The following screenshot shows an optimistic scenario with conditional formatting:

	Turnover CAGR	TGR	WACC
Optimistic	6.0%	5.5%	9.0%
Base Case	4.5%	5.0%	10.5%
Pessimistic	3.0%	4.5%	12.0%
Optimistic ▼	6.0%	5.5%	9.0%
SHARE PRICE	222.4		

The values for the Optimistic scenario now display the conditional format. That is because the currently selected scenario in our **Combo Box** is the Optimistic scenario. The share price is 222.4. Now, select the Pessimistic scenario.

The following screenshot shows the Pessimistic scenario with conditional formatting:

	Turnover CAGR	TGR	WACC
Optimistic	6.0%	5.5%	9.0%
Base Case	4.5%	5.0%	10.5%
Pessimistic	3.0%	4.5%	12.0%
Pessimistic ▼	3.0%	4.5%	12.0%
SHARE PRICE	69.9		

The values for the `Pessimistic` scenario now display the conditional format. That is because the currently selected scenario in our **Combo Box** is the `Pessimistic` scenario. The share price is `69.9`.

Creating a simple Monte Carlo simulation model

The Monte Carlo simulation is a model that calculates the probabilities of different results in a process where there is much inherent uncertainty. The model makes use of randomly generated numbers to obtain thousands of possible results, from which a most likely outcome can be deduced. We will look at growth in free cash flow, FCFF, as well as the cost of capital, WACC, which are both integral parts of our DCF model.

Calculate the FCFF growth rates for the historical years `Y02A` to `Y05A` using the following formula:

$$\text{Y02 Growth rate} = \frac{\text{Y02FCFF}}{\text{Y01FCFF}} - 1$$

The following screenshot shows the calculated historical growth in FCFF:

(Unless otherwise specified, all financial	Units	Y01A	Y02A	Y03A	Y04A	Y05A
VALUATION						
DCF Valuation using FCFF						
EBIT		27,072	19,812	51,020	34,263	45,025
Tax Rate (%)	30.0%					
EBIT*(1-t)		18,950	13,868	35,714	23,984	31,517.79
Add: Depreciation		10,000	10,000	10,000	30,000	30,000
Change in Working Capital		-	(9,642)	(8,280)	13,290	0
Less: Capex and increase in WIP						
Free Cashflow to the Firm (FCFF)		56,022	34,038	88,454	101,536	106,543
Growth in FCFF			-39%	160%	15%	5%

Usually, Monte Carlo simulation uses thousands of repetitions. However, for illustration purposes, we will limit the number to 100. Let's take the average of FCFF historical growth.

The following screenshot shows the calculation of mean growth in FCFF:

Simulations required	100		No.	FCFF	WACC
Mean growth in FCFF	=AVERAGE('Financial Model'!F237:I237)				
WACC					
Std, Deviation of FCFF growth					
Std, Deviation of WACC					
Random Number for FCFF					
Random Number for WACC					
Growth in FCFF					
WACC					

We obtain WACC from the valuation section of our model. The following screenshot shows how:

Simulations required	100		No.	FCFF	WACC
Mean growth in FCFF	35%				
WACC	='Financial Model'!D245				
Std, Deviation of FCFF growth					
Std, Deviation of WACC					
Random Number for FCFF					
Random Number for WACC					
Growth in FCFF					
WACC					

We will assume a standard deviation of 1% each. Standard deviation is a measure of how much we expect our simulations to vary from our starting values for FCFF growth and WACC. We now create a random number generator for FCFF growth and WACC using the Excel function, RAND, for both FCFF growth and WACC.

The following screenshot shows how we create a random number generator for FCFF growth and WACC:

Simulations required	100		No.	FCFF	WACC
FCFF Y06	53853.8				
Mean growth in FCFF	3%				
WACC	10.5%				
Std, Deviation of FCFF growth	1%				
Std, Deviation of WACC	1%				
Random Number for FCFF	=RAND()				
Random Number for WACC					
Growth in FCFF					
WACC					
New FCFF					
New WACC					
Final FCFF					
Final WACC					

The RAND function generates a random number between 0 and 1. Each time Excel performs a calculation in this or another cell, the function recalculates, and another random number will be regenerated. The number, 0.83751, translates to an 83.75% chance of that value occurring.

With this set up, Excel generates 100 different results for both FCFF growth and WACC. If these results were plotted on a graph, they would follow what is called a **normal distribution**.

This is a normal distribution graph:

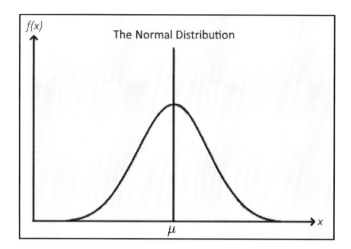

The points are clustered around a central peak. The further away a value is from the peak, the less likely it is for that value to occur. The peak represents the mean of all the values and is the most likely value of the variable. From the graph, you could select a value from the X-axis, the horizontal axis, and then trace a vertical line upward. The point at which it hits the curve gives the probability of that value occurring.

In the scenario we are creating, we are generating random probabilities and we wish to convert these to values for both FCFF growth and WACC. To do this, we use the Excel function, NORMINV. This function uses the mean, standard deviation, and probability to calculate a value for the growth in FCFF and WACC variables.

The following is a screenshot showing the NORMINV function:

Simulations required	100
Mean growth in FCFF	35%
WACC	10.5%
Std, Deviation of FCFF growth	1%
Std, Deviation of WACC	1%
Random Number for FCFF	0.169538
Random Number for WACC	0.301539
Growth in FCFF	=NORMINV(C11,C6,C8)
WACC	10.0%

We can manually force Excel to generate a fresh random number by simply pressing *F2* (**Edit**), and then *Enter*. Each time new random numbers are generated, new values are created for FCFF growth and WACC.

 Note that the values in the screenshots are different from one screenshot to the next. This is because new random numbers are being constantly generated as a result of the RAND function.

We can copy and paste these new values to another location one after the other in order to tabulate the results. We would have to do this 100 times to cover the number of simulations required by the scenario we are building. Alternatively, there is a much more efficient way to do this, using data tables.

Start off by typing 1 in a blank cell. With that cell selected, click the **Fill** icon, which is in the **Edit** group on the **Home** ribbon, and then select **Series**. This is a screenshot of the selection of **Fill>Series**:

A **Series** dialog box opens up. Select **Columns** in the **Series in** field, enter the **Step value** as 1, and the **Stop value** as 100. This is a screenshot of the **Series** dialog box:

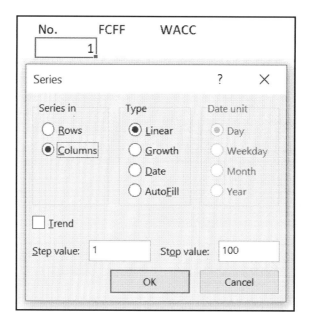

When you press **OK**, a series from 1 to 100 is generated down the column, starting with the number 1 you typed earlier. Now, create the first iteration by linking the growth in FCFF to the cell beside the number 1.

This is a screenshot showing how growth in FCFF is linked to our new table:

Simulations required	100	No.	FCFF	WACC
		1	=C13	
Mean growth in FCFF	35%	2		
WACC	10.5%	3		
Std, Deviation of FCFF growth	1%	4		
Std, Deviation of WACC	1%	5		
		6		
Random Number for FCFF	0.846634	7		
Random Number for WACC	0.350211	8		
Growth in FCFF	36.1%	9		
WACC	10.2%	10		
		11		

Then, link the WACC in the same fashion. This is a screenshot showing how WACC is linked to our new table:

Simulations required	100	No.	FCFF	WACC
		1	35.1%	=C14
Mean growth in FCFF	35%	2		
WACC	10.5%	3		
Std, Deviation of FCFF growth	1%	4		
Std, Deviation of WACC	1%	5		
		6		
Random Number for FCFF	0.511692	7		
Random Number for WACC	0.345056	8		
Growth in FCFF	35.1%	9		
WACC	10.1%	10		
		11		
		12		

We will now use **Data Table** to populate our new table with values for Growth in FCFF and WACC. Highlight all the cells in the new table, and then go to the **Forecast** group under the **Data** ribbon and select **What-If Analysis**, followed by **Data Table**. In the **Data Table** dialog box that opens up, ignore **Row input cell**.

For **Column input cell**, select any empty cell outside the table. This screenshot shows the selection of an empty cell outside the table as **Column input cell**:

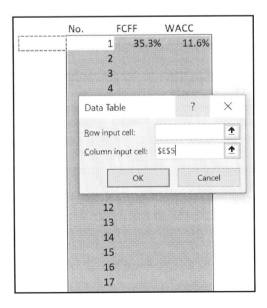

When you click **OK**, the table is populated with 100 iterations of `Growth in FCFF` and `WACC`, as shown in the following screenshot:

No.	FCFF	WACC
1	35.8%	10.6%
2	34.6%	10.7%
3	35.0%	10.6%
4	36.1%	10.8%
5	35.9%	10.3%
6	35.3%	11.6%
7	34.2%	11.7%
8	34.2%	10.7%
9	35.5%	10.1%
10	37.5%	12.2%
11	35.7%	10.9%
12	34.6%	11.2%
13	32.9%	9.5%
Down to 100	35.2%	11.5%
15	35.2%	10.3%
16	37.0%	11.2%
17	35.7%	11.8%
18	35.7%	11.0%
19	34.3%	9.5%

comps	⊕

We then obtain the most likely value for growth in FCFF, given our assumptions, by taking the average of the 100 iterations of FCFF growth. This screenshot illustrates how we arrive at new growth in FCFF:

Simulations required	100	No.	FCFF	WACC
		1	35.3%	10.7%
Mean growth in FCFF	35%	2	36.9%	9.7%
WACC	10.5%	3	34.0%	10.6%
Std, Deviation of FCFF growth	1%	4	35.2%	12.2%
Std, Deviation of WACC	1%	5	35.9%	9.0%
		6	35.3%	11.2%
Random Number for FCFF	0.601702	7	35.9%	10.7%
Random Number for WACC	0.581665	8	34.7%	10.9%
Growth in FCFF	35.3%	9	34.5%	11.1%
WACC	10.7%	10	35.0%	11.5%
		11	35.6%	12.7%
New Growth in FCFF	=AVERAGE(G5:G104)	12	35.8%	10.0%
New WACC		13	37.7%	11.2%
		14	34.7%	11.1%
		15	34.9%	10.4%
		16	34.8%	9.8%
		17	35.7%	11.5%
		18	36.2%	9.1%
		19	36.5%	9.9%

The most likely value for WACC is the average of the 100 iterations of WACC. The following screenshot illustrates how we arrive at a new WACC:

Simulations required	100	No.	FCFF	WACC
		1	35.3%	11.8%
Mean growth in FCFF	35%	2	35.4%	10.6%
WACC	10.5%	3	34.5%	11.0%
Std, Deviation of FCFF growth	1%	4	33.7%	10.7%
Std, Deviation of WACC	1%	5	36.7%	11.5%
		6	35.6%	8.9%
Random Number for FCFF	0.588018	7	36.7%	9.4%
Random Number for WACC	0.894277	8	35.5%	10.4%
Growth in FCFF	35.3%	9	35.0%	9.5%
WACC	11.8%	10	34.8%	9.6%
		11	35.6%	8.5%
New Growth in FCFF	35.0%	12	34.9%	11.0%
New WACC	-AVERAGE(H5:H104	13	34.7%	9.4%
	AVERAGE(**number1**, [number2], …)	14	34.7%	11.0%
		15	34.5%	10.2%

We will now take our new values for growth in FCFF and WACC and substitute them into our valuation model. The following screenshot shows how to do this:

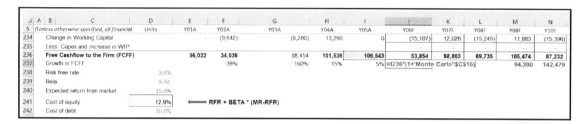

We then substitute for WACC in our formula for `Terminal Value`, as seen here:

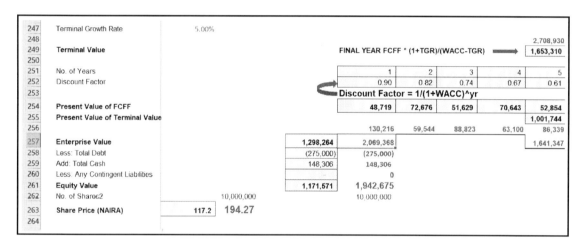

We recalculate the present values for the `FCFF` for the forecast years and the terminal value, the net present value, and so on, to arrive at an `Enterprise Value` of N'(000)`2,069,368`, an `Equity Value`, market capitalization, of N'(000) `1,942,675`, and eventually a `Share Price (NAIRA)` of `194.27`.

Summary

In this chapter, we have learned how to incorporate into your model a number of tests and procedures in order to improve the accuracy of the model. We have learned a number of basic procedures to follow in order to troubleshoot where errors are revealed in your model. We have understood the meaning of sensitivity analysis and learned how to use the direct and indirect methods. We have also learned how to display our results in a chart and to interpret them meaningfully. Finally, we learned about scenario analysis, how it differs from sensitivity analysis, and how to use it.

Financial modeling can be a complex topic, but we hope we have been able to demystify it enough to encourage you to take on what can be a very rewarding subject. It is impossible to avoid some technical content entirely, but we hope that even here, we have been able to make it less intimidating.

Another Book You May Enjoy

If you enjoyed this book, you may be interested in these other books by Packt:

Hands-On Machine Learning with Microsoft Excel 2019
Julio Cesar Rodriguez Martino

ISBN: 978-1-78934-537-7

- Use Excel to preview and cleanse datasets
- Understand correlations between variables and optimize the input to machine learning models
- Use and evaluate different machine learning models from Excel
- Understand the use of different visualizations
- Learn the basic concepts and calculations to understand how artificial neural networks work
- Learn how to connect Excel to the Microsoft Azure cloud
- Get beyond proof of concepts and build fully functional data analysis flows

Leave a review - let other readers know what you think

Please share your thoughts on this book with others by leaving a review on the site that you bought it from. If you purchased the book from Amazon, please leave us an honest review on this book's Amazon page. This is vital so that other potential readers can see and use your unbiased opinion to make purchasing decisions, we can understand what our customers think about our products, and our authors can see your feedback on the title that they have worked with Packt to create. It will only take a few minutes of your time, but is valuable to other potential customers, our authors, and Packt. Thank you!

Index

Made in the USA
Middletown, DE
31 January 2020